Sex Talks

Matthew Hosier

THANKS

To everyone who has helped me see more clearly than I would have on my own.

CONTENTS

Introduction

This is a book about sex, written by a Christian.

Everyone is talking about sex, from funny TV programs, to magazine agony aunts, your friends, your family, even your Church. In fact there are hundreds of Christian books all about the dos and don'ts around sex. So is this just one more Christian sex book in a sea of them? I hope not – I have tried to be brutally honest, giving unashamed truth to real questions asked by real young people with real desires, interests and confusion. Are you prepared to be challenged?

It might be that you are a Christian, but are confused about sex. Or you might make no claims to follow Jesus, but are interested in what it is that Christians believe. Either way, this book is for you. (Hey, it may even be that you have been trying to get that cute God-squad girl into bed and can't understand why she keeps saying "No!" This book is for you too!)

The first half of this book is based on five talks I gave at *Newday* – a large Christian youth festival that happens each summer in the UK. These five chapters try to give an overview of what the Bible teaches us about sex.

The Bible tells us that God made the world good – and in the case of the creation of man and woman, it was *very* good. But the goodness of creation was pretty soon screwed up by men and women, and this affected everything – including sex. Where this leaves us is that we have been made to enjoy God and all the good things God has made – including sex – but a lot of the time we get it all wrong.

The trouble is that in our screwed up world we normally end up getting distracted by the good things (food, clothes, possessions, and sex), and making them our gods, which then only screws things up further. Where we need to get to is an understanding that the good things are not ends in themselves but given to us so we can enjoy God more. Which means that even sex – when it is good sex – is something that is meant to help us worship God.

Hopefully the first five chapters of *Sex Talks* will help you to understand all this.

The second half of the book is made up of answers to a bunch of questions about sex that were asked by the crowd at *Newday*. These questions were sent in by text message, and were anonymous, which means some very honest questions were asked, and I have tried to be honest in my answers. I guess most people picking up this book will skip through to these questions first – no problem, but then do go back and read the first five chapters too. At the end of the book is a section on how to fight sexual temptation. Which is important.

Enjoy!

Chapter 1
Plumbing & Temples... Or, what is your body for?

Sex is obviously a very physical thing – like, d'oh – you do it with your body. It involves getting yourself completely entangled with another human being. Sex is the most intimate of human encounters, involving the exchange of warmth, and touch, and bodily fluids. Having sex with someone is to literally mingle yourself with them – a forensics guy could swab you down afterwards and find you covered in the DNA of the person you have been intimate with.

As we begin this exploration of the meaning and purpose of sex we need to start with its physical dimension. Which means we start with thinking about the body. When we have sex are we basically just functioning like plumbing? Are our bodies essentially tubes, into which we put some things and other things come out? Or is there more to it than that?

I am writing this as a Christian – a follower of Jesus Christ – who takes the Bible seriously. I believe that following Jesus and believing the Bible makes a huge difference to how we should understand sex. More than that, it makes a huge difference to how we understand our bodies – it means that we understand our bodies to be more like temples than just plumbing. This chapter is my attempt to explain that difference to you.

Sexual hang-ups?

When we read the Bible, especially the letters written by the Apostle Paul, we might get the impression that it is not too keen on sex. The general caricature of Christians is that we are sexually frigid. Lots of people would find it hard to imagine that Christians actually enjoy sex, or are any good at it. All that Bible talk of sexual immorality can just reinforce this impression.

Paul writes a lot of warnings about sexual immorality, and this might be difficult for us to understand. For starters, you might struggle with the word 'immorality'. Who gets to decide what is immoral anyway? And why just because one person thinks something is immoral does that have to affect the way that I live my life? Why should anyone but me get to define what is right or wrong with what I do with my body?

To help us understand why the Bible says what it does about sexual immorality we need to have a picture of what the world was like, that the Bible was written in. The Apostle Paul wrote his letters to churches that were in the Greek world. Greek was the language that most people spoke, and Greek culture was what shaped how people thought and acted. And lots of Greek culture was very sexually immoral.

Let's take Sparta as an example.

Sparta was an extraordinary place, even by Greek standards. It was a culture built upon steely discipline and constant training for war. The Spartans were a seriously scary bunch and their exploits in battle have become the stuff of legend. A Spartan man was expected to always be ready for a fight, able to march huge distances to get to the battle, survive off the land, kill without mercy, and never show fear. At the age of seven a Spartan boy left his parents and went to Spartan warrior school. Here he would be trained in all the things that a good Spartan needed to know. At the end of this training, the best cadets would be formed into a band called the Crypteia and go off hunting – murdering slaves as the final part of their graduation.

As well as this extreme training for war, Spartans also practiced extreme sexual training. From the age of 12 a Spartan boy was compelled to take an older, male lover. There wasn't much choice in this – it just had to be done. At the same age, a Spartan girl was considered available to any Spartan man – not to have regular intercourse, as the Spartans wanted to keep their girls 'virgins' until they got married – but for anal sex. Basically, Spartan society enforced state sanctioned pedophilia.

To us this might seem completely bizarre. It is difficult for us to imagine a society where 12 year olds are compelled by the government to have sex with older men. But for the Spartans this was normal – as normal as it would be in our culture for a 16 year-old girl to decide to start sleeping with her boyfriend.

4

New Testament sex

Sparta was an extreme case and things were somewhat different in the Greek cities Paul visited, but it gives an illustration of the kind of thing he was up against. There was a huge culture clash between what was considered normal in a place like Corinth or Ephesus and what Paul believed was right for followers of Jesus. Paul had a totally different view of God's purpose for sex from the Greek world in which he lived.

And the thing was, for those Christians who came from a Greek background, it was very difficult to break free from what they had always thought of as normal sexual behavior. So when we read what Paul writes about sexual immorality (especially in the first letter to the Corinthians) we need to understand that this is what is going on.

How does all this history relate to us? Is it outdated, or is it relevant to us, here and now?

Well, there used to be something called 'Judeo-Christian culture'. What this meant was that while not everyone was a follower of Jesus, the way that society operated was more or less along the lines set out in the Bible. People might not always have lived in sexual purity, but the basic understanding was that sex was something that was only meant to happen in marriage. Now, that culture has almost completely disappeared. Our culture today is much more like the Greek world of the New Testament. And like the converts in those first churches, we also struggle to break free from what is now considered normal sexual behavior.

Body conscious

The Greeks were like us in lots of ways. Like us, they were very body conscious – they loved looking good and were hooked on sports and pimping themselves. And like us, they lived in a highly sexualized society. Most of the time we don't even notice this – we are like goldfish swimming round a bowl and not noticing the stuff we are swimming in. But keep your eyes open and notice what is passing in front of them – look at the ads on TV and in magazines,

5

the videos on MTV, the pictures people send around on Facebook – sex is everywhere.

There is no assumption any more that sex is something that should only happen in marriage. A massive proportion of babies are born to women who are not married. Most people seem to have multiple sexual partners. And when people come to church, they pretty much always come screwed up about sex. As a pastor it sometimes feels like I spend most of my time trying to help people untangle the knots that sex has tied in their lives.

We might not be quite like the Spartans, but we are pretty much the same as the Corinthians.

If, instead of being Corinthians, we are going to be Christians, we need to get a right view of the body.

If we don't understand our bodies properly we are going to make one of two errors – either we will be like the Corinthians and reject morality, or we'll be like those caricatures of frigid Christians and reject sex. Neither of these options is good.

Body and soul

To understand sex properly we need to understand our bodies properly, which means seeing the connection between our bodies and our souls. Sex is obviously physical, but it is also very definitely spiritual. You see, what we do with our bodies is not merely physical because we are not only physical – we are embodied spirits: our body and soul are one.

Understanding this is very different from what we have been taught. What we have been taught is that the body is merely a bag made up of molecules and memories. Our bodies and minds are hugely complex, but without God in the picture we are just tubes of DNA – put food in one end, defecate out of the other, and try to cuddle up with other tubes of DNA in order to make new tubes. Our brains are simply the computer center that enables us to survive in a random world by growing food, building sewage systems, and finding someone to make babies with.

This view of the body is so dominant in our culture that it is very difficult to escape it. If it is what we believe then we will inevitably end up using our bodies like plumbing. If all we are is a piece of pipe evolved to make more pieces of pipe then we may as well follow our urges and have sex with whoever we like – only now, because of effective birth control, we can do it without having to worry about producing any pesky pieces of pipe that might get in our way and disrupt our lives.

The Bible gives us a very different account of our bodies. According to the Bible our bodies are not just tubes of DNA thrown together by the random action of evolution, but precious vessels made in the image of God.[1] This means that we are not only physical but spiritual – and that the physical and spiritual are completely intertwined. Its not like you could take a scalpel and separate the spiritual from the physical – we are embodied souls.

The body of Christ

Because our bodies are this mixture of the physical and spiritual, one of the favorite New Testament illustrations used to describe the church is 'the body'.[2] The church is not a building, or sacred space, but people who are joined together to make a "living temple."[3] The church is Christ's body, which is indwelt by his Spirit.

This means that we are to be body conscious – we are meant to treat the body of Christ with respect. Sin defiles the body, so the Bible instructs to live in a way that is pure. The way that Christians sometimes behave is like self-harming the body of Christ. We are not meant to stuff Christ's body with junk food, or make it anorexic, or cut it with a razor blade – we are meant to cherish and honor it. Jesus loves his body!

Paul writes to the Corinthians, "Do you not know that *you* are God's temple and that God's Spirit dwells in you? If anyone destroys God's temple, God will destroy him. For God's temple is holy, and you are that temple."[4] The thing to understand here is that when

---

[1] Genesis 1:27
[2] For example, see 1 Corinthians 12:12-31; Ephesians 4:1-16
[3] 1 Peter 2:4-5

7

Paul says "you" he is talking to the whole Corinthian church. In Greek, the "you" is plural – the *church* is God's temple, where his Spirit lives.

So the church is very special to Jesus – it is his temple, his body. He loves it, so we'd better look after it!

Beautiful bodies

But Paul also goes on to say that our own bodies are sacred: "Do you not know that *your* body is a temple of the Holy Spirit within you, whom you have from God? You are not your own, for you were bought with a price. So glorify God in your body."[5] In this case, the "your" is singular – Paul is speaking to the Corinthians as individuals. This means that just as we are meant to treat the body of Christ – the church – with respect, we need to be careful what we do with our own bodies. If you are a Christian your body isn't just yours – Jesus has bought it, at a great cost, on the cross, and the Spirit of God is at work in you. So what you do with your body really matters to God – it matters what you do sexually, or if you self-harm or abuse your body with drugs.

A lot of us have body issues. Lots of us don't treat our bodies as precious to God and beautiful in his sight, but as something that is ugly and painful.

Is there anyone who looks in the mirror and wouldn't like to change something about their physical appearance? We have all done it – all of us feel that our hair is too straight or too curly, our noses are too big or too small, that we are too short or too tall. Many people live in mental agony over the state of their body. Some people really hate their bodies. Self-harm, eating disorders, and just plain old embarrassment are commonplace. Why? Because we don't really believe our bodies are beautiful – but God does.

If you think your body is a piece of junk you are likely to treat it that way. A student at my church told me that after being rejected

---

[4] 1 Corinthians 3:16-17
[5] 1 Corinthians 6:19-20

by a guy she liked she went out and kissed two other guys just to try and get a sense of worth and affirmation through sex. I've heard so many women say things like, "I thought I was ugly and worthless, so I made myself sexually available to anyone who would have me just so I could feel some love." This is tragic – and it's not just the girls. I've known so many guys who live in constant terror of other people pointing out their physical imperfections, and so are always putting up a front to try and look like something they are not. Many men get their sense of masculinity and power through sexual conquests. This is sad.

Rather than considering our bodies as junk, the Apostle Paul tells the Corinthians (and us) that we are to glorify God in our bodies. What does this mean?

Glorifying God in our bodies

We might get an idea of what glorifying God in our bodies looks like when we look at those people who are totally uninhibited in their bodies. Think of a great athlete, who can do things with their body that would be impossible for the rest of us – the power, speed, and grace with which a truly gifted athlete can pass a ball, jump a hurdle or turn a somersault. When I see athletes like this it always excites me and it feels somehow spiritual, because what these guys are doing feels something like worship – there is a discipline and a freedom about their bodies which just seems to shout out praise to the creator, even if they don't know who he is.

Something similar goes on with little kids. Young children clearly don't have the same kind of skills and power as trained athletes, but there can be a bodily freedom in children that is similarly glorious. Last summer I set up a sprinkler on our lawn and my kids spend hours jumping over it – and it was glorious! They were so completely lacking in self-consciousness. They were just enjoying their bodies and what their bodies could do. They weren't worrying about how they looked. They weren't having to check themselves out in a mirror every few minutes. They weren't worried about who might see them. They were just being glorious!

To glorify God in our bodies means that we have something of the athletes devotion and the child's freedom before God. It means we use our bodies in a way that is pleasing to him and has him cheering us on. It means we are not inhibited before him but stand confident and happy in his presence. It means we truly believe that God looks at our bodies and thinks they are beautiful.

Why is sex such a big deal?

If we are going to glorify God in our beautiful bodies then how we behave sexually is massively important.

Sex goes to the very heart of what it means to be human. It goes to the heart of our relationship with God and with other people. Who you have sex with and who you don't have sex with is very important!

Think about it – none of us would be here without sex. That might be a pretty gross thought, as thinking about the fact that your parents had sex *is* pretty gross, but its true. Even if you were born as the result of IVF that was still in some ways sexual – your biological father had to provide a sperm sample; his sperm and your mothers egg had to get mixed up together. There is no way around it: No sex = No you.

How we think and act sexually is also important in that so much of where we get our sense of identity from is tied up with our sexuality. We all tend to define ourselves by sexually conditioned terms: *virgin, married, gay, straight, bi...*

But as well as being partly inevitable, this way of identifying ourselves *sexually* is also massively limiting. As followers of Jesus, it should be our identity *in Christ* that defines us over and above everything else. It is this identity – "I am in Christ!" – that then shapes how we think about everything else, including sex.

And here's the thing – How we behave sexually is not an indifferent matter. It has a huge impact upon the body – both our own bodies, and the body of the church.

A case study in thinking about the body

It is in Paul's first letter to the Corinthians that we get one of the clearest biblical messages about how we should think about sex, especially in chapters 5 to 7.

In these chapters Paul applies body language to the individual but always has the bigger body – the church – in view. Paul lists some things that believers *cannot* do. The reason that followers of Jesus cannot do these things is because they deny the sacrifice of Christ, which cleanses us from our sin. They are also things that damage community – they are the kind of actions that weaken relationships, break down trust, and start fights. And, most importantly, they are also things that undermine the witness of the church, as non-believers look on and say, "You Christians are no different from the rest of us – you are all hypocrites."

The things Paul lists include non-sexual sins: idolatry, stealing, greed, drunkenness, dishonesty, slander. But there is a particular focus on sex: sexual immorality, adultery, homosexuality, prostitution. Basically, Paul is saying that followers of Christ must not be involved in any sexual activity outside marriage.

Why?

Because of the change Christ has worked in us
If you are a Christian you have been born again. You have been raised to new life in Christ. Your body is a temple of the Holy Spirit. Which means you can't take something that is now sacred to God and use it in a way that is impure.

The Corinthians were saying, "All things are lawful for me"[6] but this was a twisting of grace. As those who have received the grace of God anything is permissible for us, so long as it lines up with us being "in Christ." In the end the question is not whether something is *lawful* but whether it is *good*. Does what you do reflect what Jesus has done in you? Does what you do help you to love Jesus more and become more like him? If it doesn't, don't do it.

---

[6] 1 Corinthians 6:12

Because Christ is our master

Christians are not to be mastered by anything but Jesus. Often, what is described as 'freedom' is actually slavery. This is especially true when it comes to things like sex. It might look like freedom to indulge all your sexual desires, but if this means you are in reality a slave to your sexual desires you are not really free.

Paul writes, "You are not your own, for you were bought with a price."[7] By becoming a Christian you have chosen to submit yourself completely to Jesus and his will. This is why the New Testament often describes Christians as *slaves* of Christ. Now, you don't just get to follow the urges of your body – you do what your master requires of you – and this includes living in sexual purity.

Because in Christ we will be raised to new life

Paul quotes a Corinthian slogan, "Food is meant for the stomach and the stomach for food."[8] It seems that the Corinthians were taking a slogan about food and applying it to sex – saying, in effect, "The body is meant for sex and sex for the body. And what we're doing with our bodies doesn't matter, because God is going to destroy them anyway."

If you think the body is basically trash, which is going to get destroyed so that your spirit can be liberated, then it really doesn't matter what you do with your body. But this is wrong!

It is wrong because our bodies are not meant for destruction but resurrection! This is why Paul writes, "The body is not meant for sexual immorality, but for the Lord, and the Lord for the body. And God raised the Lord and will also raise us up by his power."[9] If you think that Jesus died only to 'save your soul' you haven't understood the gospel. Jesus died to save *you* – body and soul. Your body isn't just a lump of useless DNA that is going to get burned up – it is something beautiful that God made and Jesus died for.

Just as Jesus was raised from the dead, when he returns we will be raised with him. Jesus was raised to life with a physical body – but without the limitations we experience at the moment in our

---

[7] 1 Corinthians 6:19
[8] 1 Corinthians 6:13
[9] 1 Corinthians 6:13-14

physical bodies. The Christian hope is that one day we will get bodies like his. Bodies that will still be physical, but will never age or get sick or die. We will live in a new heavens and earth that are *physical* as well as spiritual. Our bodies are precious!

Who are you joined to?

While we can look ahead with excitement to the day when we get our resurrection bodies, the reality is that if we are followers of Jesus we are already members of his body. We somehow have become joined to him.

Being joined to Christ in this way then defines what else we can join our body to – which explains what Paul says about prostitutes in 1 Corinthians 6. Prostitution was rife in Corinth and the Greek and Roman world. It is also rife in our world. It is no harder to find a prostitute in any town in our world than it was in Corinth.

Going to prostitutes was standard practice in Corinth, but it is not standard practice for Christians! It is just not possible for a Christian to join himself to a prostitute. How can you join with someone who is not herself destined for resurrection? How can you deny your primary joining – which is to Jesus?

Flee sexual immorality

We are to flee *all* sexual immorality, because sexual sin is different from other sins. Paul writes, "Every other sin a person commits is outside the body, but the sexually immoral person sins against his own body."[10] Sexual sin is different from other sins because it has a much bigger impact in defining our relationships with others – and as members of the body of Christ, being a Christian is all about relationships.

Think about it this way... Sex is good, holy and desirable within marriage, because sex in some way defines the relationship between husband and wife. Husband and wife are meant to have

---

[10] 1 Corinthians 6:18

sex together, and this sexual relationship is meant to help them live together fruitfully, faithfully and sacrificially. Sex in marriage is meant to result in kids – without sex there wouldn't be any children. But parents are not meant to have sex with their kids – that is not good, holy and desirable – it is despicable and wrong. So the relationship between parents and their children is defined by the fact that this is *not* a sexual relationship, even though it is a relationship that would never have existed if there hadn't been sex.

Get it?

The fact that some relationships are meant to be sexual and others are not then spreads out beyond the immediate biological family unit. Whenever we have sex with someone we are not meant to it screws things up, and when things get screwed up sexually they tend to get more screwed up than they would be by anything else. If someone who is part of a church has an affair with someone else in the church this screws things up far more thoroughly than other kinds of sin because sex is more central to how our relationships are defined than anything else.

We are also to flee sexual sin because it places us under the mastery of another, when Christ is our master and has purchased us at cost. Paul says that if you sleep with a prostitute you become "one body with her."[11] When you have sex with someone you in some way come under their authority because part of you sticks to them, and part of them sticks to you. This is good and right when it is husband and wife, but wrong when it is anyone else. And the fact is, you don't even have to be physically sleeping with someone to be mastered by them – if you are stuck on porn then it has become your master, and it is not meant to be.

Sexual sin is also a denial of the goodness of the body. This might sound strange, because people will often describe 'sexual liberty' in terms of it being like doing sport – as something that is just a healthy physical activity. But this simply reflects a wrong understanding of what God created our bodies for. If we understand that we are meant to glorify God in our bodies we will understand this means that doing anything that doesn't glorify God

---

[11] 1 Corinthians 6:16

is actually to sin against our bodies, and deny their goodness. If our bodies are going to be raised to new life in Christ, and we are going to reign with him forever, then we shouldn't screw around with our bodies now. If our bodies really are temples of the Spirit we need to treat them with incredible respect.

Not just plumbing...

I hope that I have been able to convince you that your body is a long way from just being a tube of plumbing, and that this must have a big impact on how you think about sex.

Let's finish this chapter by looking at a scene from the last book of the Bible, the book of Revelation. In Revelation 5, the apostle John has a vision of heaven, with the Lamb of God – Jesus – being worshipped by heavenly creatures. These sing a song of worship to Jesus:

> *"Worthy are you to take the scroll*
> *and to open its seals,*
> *for you were slain, and by your blood you ransomed people for God*
> *from every tribe and language and people and nation,*
> *and you have made them a kingdom and priests to our God,*
> *and they shall reign on the earth."*

Do you see what this song says?

What Jesus has done for us didn't come cheap, but at great cost – he died for us. And what Jesus has achieved for us isn't cheap either, but magnificent and amazing – we are going to reign with Christ forever!

Now, if you can grasp the scale of what all this means you are not going to screw things up by screwing around with sex. If you can really get it in your guts that your body is not just the result of random acts of evolution but the beautifully planned handiwork of God you are going to think carefully about what you do with it. If you catch hold of the vision of Revelation and see that your destiny is to reign with Christ forever, and to serve as a priest before him you are not going to want to do anything that compromises your relationship with him.

Your body is not just plumbing. It is a beautiful temple for God.

Chapter 2
Doing it like mammals on the Discovery Channel... Or, what is the purpose of sex?

We've spent some time thinking about our bodies and how amazing and loved by God they are. But what, really, is the point of sex? Why do we have these urges? And what are they meant to achieve?

If our bodies are temples rather than just plumbing, then there must be some holy purpose to sex. It cannot be a case of sex being a bit like going to the gym – something we do for physical exercise and release. Sex is far more all-consuming than that. It gets hold of our minds as much as our genitals. But many people treat it like a recreational sport – do it with as many people as you can; get your rocks off to some porn; assess other people by how much you'd like to screw them on a scale of 1 to 10.

If this casual attitude to sex is inappropriate for people who know they are living, walking, talking temples, we need to get some biblical clarity about what sex is for. Thankfully, a lot of good people have given a lot of good thought to this over the past 2,000 years so we are not starting from a blank sheet. In distilling what the Bible teaches about the purpose of sex the teaching of the Church over the centuries can be summed up in three words: Fruitful, Faithful and Sacrificial.

Let's look at these three, one at a time...

Sex should be fruitful

How many children?

If the population of a country is to remain stable, every woman needs to have 2.1 babies. (The reason it is not exactly 2 is because of childhood mortality.) Of course, no woman has point one of a baby – 2.1 is an average. This is what demographers call the *replacement rate*. The number of babies that women actually have is called the *total fertility rate*, and in many western countries this number is way below 2.1. For example, in Poland it is only 1.23.

This means the Poles might become extinct sometime in the next few decades.

More interestingly, it shows how our attitudes to children have changed. Lots more kids are growing up without any brothers or sisters around than used to be the case, and lots of woman are choosing not to have any children at all.

Add to this the fact that people are living longer and we can predict some very strange changes in society. By 2050 the majority of children in Europe will have no brothers or sisters, no cousins, aunts or uncles. But they will have three to four grandparents and one to three great-grandparents still alive.

This is very different from how human society has operated throughout the rest of history. What the human race has been used to is being part of a family, and community, where there are lots of children and young people, fewer adults, and hardly any old folks. With the changes in breeding habits we are now seeing we are going to have to get used to living in a world where the family is very small, but very stretched – rather than having brothers and sisters and cousins to hang out with, it will just be your parents and grandparents and great-grandparents.

This has huge practical implications. It has huge implications for pension provision and care for the elderly. I guess this isn't something you spend too much time thinking and worrying about, but bear with me a minute and see if you can answer these questions – How will pensions get paid if there are no younger people to produce money? How will the elderly get cared for if they outnumber younger people? What will life be like when your great-grandparents and grandparents and parents have all died, and there are no children or grandchildren coming through to replace them? Sounds kinda lonely...

Kid conflict

It seems to me that there are a lot of conflicting attitudes to children in our society. On one hand, we live in a society that idolizes children. Kids aren't allowed to do anything dangerous anymore – or anything that *looks* like it might be dangerous. Parents keep their kids cooped up inside watching TV and getting fat on coke and pizza because they are too scared of the traffic, and the pedophiles, and the plague to let them play outside. And too many parents treat their kids like little gods.

Have you ever seen a young child in a supermarket screaming at its mother to put more sugar in her shopping cart, and the mother doing so in order to keep her child quiet? That's an example of treating your child like a little god.

But on the other hand, children are also often seen as a burden. One of the reasons people are having fewer babies, or starting families later in life, is because children are seen as something that stops adults from doing all the things they want to do. Adults have so many important things to do – they have got to build their careers and having kids gets right in the way of that. They also need to make sure they have plenty of time to pursue all their leisure activities, and its not so easy to go out drinking or climbing mountains if there are kids holding you back. Kids just get so in the way!

Babies = Blessing

The biblical view of children is very different from our world's. The Bible sees children as a gift from God and as a sign of his blessing. We see this right at the beginning of the story in Genesis chapter 1. The story is about God creating the world, and making it ready for Adam and Eve to live in it. But where all this amazing creative work leads is to God pronouncing a blessing, and that was a blessing to make babies: *And God blessed them. And God said to them, "Be fruitful and multiply and fill the earth."*[12]

---

[12] Genesis 1:28

In the Bible blessings are very powerful. They are not like when someone in church says, "Bless you" as a kind of alternative to saying "Goodbye." In the Bible when someone pronounces a blessing stuff really happens. And when it is God who is making the blessing you can bet there is power involved. So God blessed Adam and Eve and told them to get on with making babies. They were to be fruitful.

This attitude of seeing children as a sign of God's blessing continues throughout the Bible. For instance Psalm 127:3 says, *Sons are a heritage from the Lord, children a reward from him.* In the Old Testament just about the worst thing that could happen to you was to not have kids.

Maybe you feel your life is boring, or a waste of time. Maybe your parents have let you down, or worse. If this is the case it is important you understand that you are not just an accident. You are not just a lump of flesh uselessly sitting around consuming the earth's resources. You exist because of blessing! If God had never pronounced that first blessing over Adam and Eve you wouldn't be here today. This means you can be confident that the blessing of God in your life is real – and powerful.

Sex = Babies

It is pretty obvious that sex is meant to result in babies – that's what all that equipment we carry around with us is for! But because we now have efficient contraception, we can forget the obvious, and many people seem to think men have been given penises and women vaginas simply as recreational items.

However, the Bible is clear that sex is meant to result in children. This doesn't mean that sex is meant to be some kind of clinical activity, like a vet performing artificial insemination on a cow. Sex is relational – which we'll look at more when we consider the ways in which it is meant to be faithful and sacrificial – but it is also meant to be fruitful.

There will, of course, be times when sex is not fruitful, and babies don't result, because of infertility. For those couples who experience infertility, this is a really tough thing to handle, which takes a lot of time and love to work through. But generally speaking we can say that sex is intended for the purpose of reproduction.

Biblically speaking, marriage is the place in which a man and a woman are joined together as one, and this joining must include "loining" – if a couple don't have sex they're not really married. And if a couple are having sex, they should be open to the possibility of achieving the end for which sex is intended – children. This is not to say that we should not use contraception. But it does mean that the possibility of making a baby should not be permanently excluded from sexual activity. If we choose to permanently exclude the possibility of reproduction from sex we choose to exclude ourselves from the blessing promised us by God in having children.

When God joined Adam and Eve together he created the first building blocks of community. It was a community that was meant to grow, and it grew by having children. This first marriage provides the pattern for all subsequent marriages – marriage is meant to grow community, and it does so by producing children.

Sex is meant to be fruitful.

Sex should be faithful

It is not only in our attitude to children that western society is going through huge change. Marriage itself is under attack as never before. In the UK now most adults are unmarried, something which has never before been the case. It used to be taken for granted that once people became adults they would get married, they would have kids, and they would stay married. Now the expectation is that you might live with someone for a while, or just sleep around while still living at home with your mom doing all your cooking and ironing like you are a little kid, even if you are actually 35! Of course, lots of people do get married, but lots of people also get divorced.

Things are not as straightforward as they used to be.

For the Christian there are some positive reasons for not marrying. Staying single – and celibate – is not a disaster for a Christian, because all Christians are part of a family that is bigger and more important than our flesh and blood families. All Christians are children of God, and have countless brothers and sisters in Christ. Everyone of us is also meant to experience fruitfulness because as Christians we are grafted into the vine that is Christ, which means we will be fruitful.[13] Having babies is just one way of being fruitful, not the only (or even the most important) way.

But when it comes to sex we can see that the decline in the number of people marrying and staying married reflects a decrease in faithfulness. And this is not good.

The reality is that we are afraid of making commitments. We prefer to keep our options open. This attitude might be because we worry that if we commit to one thing a better thing might come along later and we will end up disappointed and miserable. How do you know that if you commit to marry someone who you think is pretty fit, and funny, and talented that a year or two down the line you won't meet someone who looks better and makes you laugh more and earns more money?! This is a real issue for us because our consumer society trains us to always keep our options open and expect to trade up to a better model when one comes along. No-one expects to drive the same car their whole lives, or listen to the same mp3 player, or wear the same shoes. That would be just so last year.

The trouble is that the attitudes driven into us by our consumer society are not helpful when it comes to building happy and healthy relationships. They do nothing to encourage faithfulness. Can you imagine a company like Nike changing their advertising so it said something like, "Never buy a new pair of trainers from us again! Those ones we sold you two years ago are still really cool!"? It's not going to happen.

And where this leaves us is bouncing from one relationship to another, always looking for perfection, and always being disappointed.

---

[13] John 15:5

Another reason we might be afraid of making commitments is that so many of us have experienced what happens when a commitment is broken. If your experience growing up was of all the people who were meant to be most trustworthy letting you down, it's not surprising if you have trust issues. If your mom walked out on your dad, and you never saw a relationship that lasted, why should you want to try and make any lasting commitments yourself? And even if this wasn't your experience, the fact that it was the experience of lots of your friends will have left you burnt about commitment.

The reality is, we live in a "divorce culture" where every one of us is affected by the general lack of faithfulness we see all around us. As well as making us nervous of commitments, this divorce culture also makes us look for legal guarantees. When we can't trust people we need to have a contract with them, so we can sue them and screw them if they try to screw us. This is why we live in a society with evermore rules and regulations, and stupid warnings on cups of coffee saying "This will be hot." Where there is a lack of trust – a lack of faithfulness – then all we have to rely on is the law.

God is faithful

Throughout the Bible the relationship between God and his people is described as one in which God is faithful, even if often his people are not. This relationship is likened to a marriage, in which God is a faithful and jealous husband pursuing his straying bride. This "marriage" gives us some of the most shocking language in the Bible. For example, chapter 16 of Ezekiel describes God's people as a whore, and explains with terrifying intensity how judgment will be poured out on them as a result. But the story doesn't end with judgment – it ends with the faithful love of our faithful God: *I will atone for all you have done.*[14]

It is God's example of faithfulness that we are to pursue in our relationships, and especially in marriage. Where sex is involved there needs to be more faithfulness. Why? Because of what sex is meant to produce. Part of this is the production of babies, because sex is meant to be fruitful, and children do best when raised by

---

[14] Ezekiel 16:63

parents who are faithful to one another. But sex is also meant to produce a deepening of relationship between a couple. Sex is the most personal thing you can do – it requires complete self-disclosure – and this kind of intimacy deserves the protection of faithfulness.

Sex isn't just a matter of connecting pieces of plumbing.

If God is faithful, we have got to come to the place where we believe he can help us to be faithful too, and that this is actually the best way to live. God's faithfulness is the antidote to our consumerism. Think about it – God could definitely have chosen a better model than me, but choose me he did, and he will never let me go. If God treats me like this, then I must be able to reflect the same kind of faithfulness in relationships without always worrying about whether I have made the right decision. This is why one of my favorite expressions to sum up how I feel about my marriage is, "I've settled it in my heart." Faithfulness is a decision I have made, and by the grace of God is a decision I can keep. It is settled.

God's faithfulness is also the antidote to the nervousness we feel about commitment because of the way we have seen others break their commitments. In the end, our model needs to be Jesus, not anyone else. When we start to get a handle on the faithfulness of Jesus – a faithfulness that went so far it ended at the cross – we can start to live faithfully ourselves. We've got to believe that the power of his faithfulness at work in us will enable us to live faithfully, even if all our human models have failed.

Faithful marriage is the bedrock of society. Faithfulness in marriage extends to faithfulness from parents towards their children, and from the family to neighbors, and from neighbors to the neighborhood. This means sex should be part of the glue of faithfulness, and not a wrecking bar that shatters it.

Be faithful – don't have sex with anyone you're not married to; and if you are married, faithfully (and regularly!) make love to your partner.

Sex should be sacrificial

Watching the ~~porn~~ music videos on MTV, you'd get the idea that sex is all about taking. But as soon as you get involved with another real, flesh and blood, human being, you discover that for any relationship to succeed requires at least as much giving as taking. In fact, what the Bible calls us to is the giving of complete sacrifice.

I have already argued that sex should be fruitful and faithful, and this means it is something that should be kept exclusively for marriage. That sex should also be sacrificial raises the stakes on this even higher.

According to the Bible, marriage should be a place where we experience God's mercy and grace, and it is also the setting in which we are to display mercy and grace to another. The model scripture gives to us for this kind of marriage is the relationship between Christ and the church:

> *Husbands, love your wives, just as Christ loved the church and gave himself up for her to make her holy, cleansing her by the washing with water through the word, and to present her to himself as a radiant church, without stain or wrinkle or any other blemish, but holy and blameless. In this same way, husbands ought to love their wives as their own bodies. He who loves his wife loves himself. After all, no-one ever hated his own body, but he feeds and cares for it, just as Christ does the church – for we are members of his body. For this reason a man will leave his father and mother and be united to his wife, and the two will become one flesh. This is a profound mystery – but I am talking about Christ and the church. However, each one of you also must love his wife as he loves himself, and the wife must respect her husband.*[15]

In Christ's relationship with the church there is a complete and total giving. Jesus gave himself for the church – he went to the cross for her; he sacrificed himself for her; he died for her. What is extraordinary about this passage in Ephesians is the way that it says that the way Christ acted is the way husbands should act towards their wives. It is made very clear. Husbands are to love their wives *just* as Christ loved the church. Just like Jesus sacrificed

---

[15] Ephesians 5:25-33

himself for his church, husbands are to sacrifice themselves for their wives.

This is the model for human marriage – it is about sacrifice. This is very different from how people often approach relationships. Our culture conditions us to think about ourselves and our own happiness and rights. Jesus teaches us to sacrifice.

Sacrifice is absolute. It is life and death. It is an unconditional giving of ourselves. It is an unreserved entrusting of ourselves to another person. It is on this basis that we should enter into marriage. People get married for all sorts of different reasons: because of romantic love; because of lust; because it is "the right thing to do"; because the woman has got pregnant... There is greater or lesser validity to all these reasons but when a Christian enters marriage the primary reason should be a determination to serve another person completely for the rest of their life.

And just in case you're wondering, this isn't a one way street. The focus in Ephesians 5 is on the way a husband is to love his wife, but the wife is also to respect her husband. Just as the church honors Jesus, so a wife should honor her husband, and that kind of respect requires sacrifice too.

Understanding this has a profound impact upon how we approach sex. What should be obvious is that sex is not meant to be about self-assertion. Sex too often is a selfish thing. When we talk about sex we too often talk about "our needs." And sex too often is about power – the politics of the bedroom – as husband and wife either demand, offer, or refuse sex as a means of control and manipulation.

Sex in marriage should not to be like this. Rather than being demanding, sex should be sacrificial – an offering to one another. This sacrificial offering raises sex from the level of being purely biological and makes it spiritual. It becomes an act in which husband and wife seek out one another's souls as well as one another's bodies. It becomes an act in which the "one flesh" bond between husband and wife is affirmed and strengthened. It becomes something which once again truly enjoys the blessing of God. Sacrificial sex is life affirming. It is good, holy and pure.

Sacrificial sex is not merely a physical act – it is a complete giving of one to another. It is truly becoming one flesh.

This is how sex should be, and that means that sex is something that should only take place within marriage. A sexual relationship is a serious thing. It is meant to involve a lifelong pursuit of one another. It is meant to be exclusive – between one man and one woman, until death.

And we see in Ephesians 5 the particular things husband and wife are to offer one another if they are to reflect the relationship between Christ and the church. In verse 33 it says that the husband must love his wife and the wife must respect her husband. These are the fundamental emotional requirements of a successful marriage. For a wife the most devastating thing she could hear her husband say is, "I respect you but I don't love you," while the most devastating thing a husband could hear from his wife is, "I love you but I don't respect you." Wives need to know the unconditional, tender, strong love of their husbands, and husbands need to know the genuine respect of their wives.

This is important when it comes to sex because an unloved wife will not be a liberated lover. And a disrespected husband is not going to have any confidence in bed.

Sex is meant to be sacrificial. It is to reflect the relationship between Christ and his church. It is only within marriage that such a relationship can exist – a relationship that is exclusive, life-long, and entirely self-giving.

So how far is too far...?

If you've stuck with me this far, hopefully you are getting a clearer understanding of the significance of sex, and of the significance of marriage. It might be, though, that you still want to ask the question, "Ok, but how far can I go with my girl/boyfriend before we're married and having full sex?"

This is the wrong question!

The question you really need to be asking is how does the way that you act honor the body of Christ? Our aim shouldn't be to draw some kind of line and then push as close to that line as possible. Our aim should be to do what is most pleasing to Jesus – and that means sex being faithful, fruitful and sacrificial.

Chapter 3
I kissed a girl and I liked it... Or, what we should think about homosexuality

First it was Britney and Madonna making out on stage, then, a few years later, it was Lady Gaga getting in on the act. The message is clear: All the cool girls like a bit of lesbian action.

30 years ago homosexuality was something that was hidden and largely disapproved of. Today being gay, lesbian or bi is considered increasingly normal – even desirable. And even among people who would describe themselves as straight there is increasing experimentation with same-sex relationships. Teenage girls are just as likely to kiss another girl as they are to make out with a boy.

So what should we think about homosexuality?

Who do you think you are?

One of the most significant strategies of the gay movement has been to blur the distinctions between what sex we are and to categorize everyone along a more slippery definition of "gender." Rather than simply being male or female, we are now meant to describe ourselves by our sexual orientation and preferences. And the way in which we identify ourselves sexually becomes the most important thing about who we are.

So, in answer to the question, "What are you?" we now tend to quickly jump to gender descriptions: Gay, lesbian, bi, trans, straight.

This is where Christians need to be clear – because who we are is *not* defined primarily by our sexuality: Our culture might try to define us according to our sexual preferences; the Bible does not.

Sexual orientation is not the single most important aspect of what it means to be human! The difference between the Bible and our culture on this is striking. The Bible never asks anyone to fill out a form on which they need to tick a box which most closely reflects their sexual orientation. The Bible never says, so-and-so was a straight man, or such-and-such was a bi woman. It simply describes men and women, and the change worked in them by the presence of God.

But this doesn't mean that our sex is unimportant. It is vital that God has created us as male and female. This is a central aspect of what it means to be human. We are made in the image of God, and we reflect God as male and female.[16] The Bible also makes it clear that men and women need one another – that we are mutually dependent upon each other.[17]

So a problem with homosexuality is that it blurs the God-created distinction between male and female by saying there isn't really such a thing as male and female, just a range of sexual orientations. It also severs the mutual dependence between male and female by saying two women or two men can make as equally a valid relationship as a man and a woman. And underlying these two problems is the bigger one that homosexuality reduces the way we define ourselves to sexual orientation, which the Bible never does.

For a Christian, the thing that is most defining about who we are is our relationship with Jesus. One of the favorite ways for the New Testament to describe who Christians are is to say that we are "in Christ."[18] If you are a Christian this is the most important thing about you! Where you were born, what color your skin is, or what your social status is are not that important. What counts is that you are in Christ – he has made you new, he loves you, and you will be with him forever! Compared to this, defining yourself by your sexual orientation is pretty lame.

Nature or Nurture?

In the debate about homosexuality a lot of heat gets generated about whether being gay is the result of nature (our DNA) or nurture (the way we were raised). This is considered important because if someone is gay because they were "born that way," then it doesn't seem fair that they should be expected to be anything but

---

[16] Genesis 1:27
[17] 1 Corinthians 11:11
[18] E.g., Galatians 6:15, 2 Corinthians 5:17

gay. However, if someone is made gay by their upbringing, then presumably they can also be "cured" of being gay.

The problem with this debate is that it is very difficult to get conclusive evidence for either side. It also makes the issue very polarized – it just leads to endless fights. And it diminishes who we actually are as humans by saying either that we are simply the product of biology, or that we are slaves to our environment.

A better way to understand ourselves is to recognize that the way in which we feel about things and understand the world is the result of both our genes and our experience and knowledge. The reality is that everyone of us has particular areas of weakness and vulnerability which are the result of both nature and nurture. It is not particularly easy to say whether my susceptibility to temptation in one area is because of the DNA my parents passed onto me, or because of the way they brought me up. It's probably a combination of the two – and what counts *now* is how I deal with that temptation.

This is why the Bible is clear that we are responsible for our own behavior. As Christians we cannot excuse our sin on the grounds that, "I can't help it – it's just how I am," or, "I can't help it – it's just how I was raised." While our DNA and our environment play a massive part in shaping who we are, neither factor removes our personal responsibility for how we act now. For the Christian, the key thing is that we are new creations, in Christ – we are born again! And this changes everything. We now have the power of God's Spirit at work in us – which is more significant than our DNA. And we have the example of Christ's life to follow – which is more meaningful than the life experiences we had growing up.

So why are some people gay? I think it is unarguable that there is a genetic element to it. Some people just are more likely to be attracted to people of the same sex for genetic reasons. However, it is also obvious that in the area of sexuality individual attitudes and actions are profoundly shaped by society as a whole – so the more that being gay is considered acceptable (or desirable) the more people are likely to experiment with being gay.

Where this leaves us is that the question of whether nature or nurture are responsible for sexual orientation is not really that interesting! The key thing is how we work out our sexuality – and as we have already seen, biblically speaking the only legitimate place for sex to happen is within marriage.

So, the real question we have to answer is this one: Can homosexuals be married?

Gay Marriage?

This is a hot issue across the western world because an increasing number of governments are allowing gay marriage in one form or another. (As I write this, New York State has just decided to legalize gay marriage, and the UK Government says it intends to.) This means that if you live somewhere where gay marriage is allowed but say that it is wrong, you could find yourself on the wrong side of the law. So we need to be really clear about what we think about this, and the best place to start is with what we have already seen marriage is meant to be about: Fruitfulness, faithfulness and sacrifice.

Fruitfulness

Marriage is meant to produce children, because sex is meant to produce children and sex is meant to be part of marriage. Obviously, this cannot be the case in a gay marriage. Baby, it takes a man and a woman to make a baby.

This means that gay marriage fails the first test of what a true marriage is. However (and this is an important point that gay couples will want to make), not all heterosexual marriages produce children. Do we say that these are not really marriage as well?

The difference here should be obvious. If a married man and woman are unable to have children because they are infertile, that is what philosophers call *accidental effect*, whereas the inability of a homosexual couple to reproduce is an essential and inevitable aspect of their relationship. Heterosexual couples can be fruitful, unless there is some biological reason preventing it, but the only way a homosexual couple can have a child is by involving a third party – by buying or borrowing someone else's eggs or sperm, which is a form of adultery.

Marriage is the basic building block of community and having children is an extension of that community. If a couple refuse to have children they fail to create community and so miss out on that aspect of God's intended plan for marriage – and I would argue that they shouldn't have got married in the first place! Gay relationships, by definition, fail to create community because they are by definition incapable of producing children. And this means they are incapable of receiving this aspect of God's blessing upon marriage.

Faithfulness

It is on the grounds of faithfulness that the strongest argument can be made in support of gay marriage. If a gay couple love each other, and are committed to each other, why shouldn't that relationship of faithfulness be recognized and celebrated just as much as would be the case for a heterosexual couple?

That is a good question! To answer it we need to be clear about how the Bible defines faithfulness. As I explained in Chapter 2, the biblical model for faithfulness is God himself – God makes promises to his people and is faithful to them. It is this example that then becomes the model for faithfulness within human marriage.

But here's the thing: The Bible always describes this kind of faithful marriage as between husband and wife. Of course, there needs to be faithfulness in all kinds of other relationships – between parents and children, between friends, between neighbors – but these relationships are different from marriage. Gay relationships can be faithful, but they do not reflect the marriage relationship between Christ and his church, which is always described in the language of male and female. This distinction between male and female is not merely a question of language – it has profound implications for how marriage partners relate to one another, as we will see when we consider the sacrificial aspect of marriage.

Sacrifice

Ephesians chapter 5 is one of the key Bible passages that helps us understand God's intention for marriage. In verse 32 Paul describes the relationship between Christ and the church (and between husband and wife) as "a profound mystery." What does this mean? Why are these relationships mysterious?

A large part of this mystery is down to the fact that the partners are so very different.

Think about the relationship between Christ and the church. There is a mystery to it! How could it be that God should be so passionate about a bunch of sinful humans? How is it that God should give himself up for us, even dying on a cross for us? How is it that God should make such great promises over his church, that he will keep us and guard us, and that he is preparing a wedding feast for us? How is it that God can say that we are his body on earth?

These things are a profound mystery!

The point Paul makes in Ephesians 5 is that the relationship between husband and wife is also mysterious, because men and women are so different. There is mystery about the way in which a man and a woman can become one flesh in marriage. There is a mystery about the way in which two people who are different can experience a greater sense of unity in this relationship than they do in any other.

We see the mystery of marriage especially worked out when a couple have a baby. We might understand the biology of how this happens, but there is still something spiritually mysterious about the way that sex can create babies. When Grace and I had our babies it felt mysterious every time. We knew how Grace had got pregnant – I mean, that didn't just happen somehow in our sleep – but that this *thing* should be the result felt utterly mysterious, magical and miraculous.

Marriage is an embracing of this mystery – it is an embracing of the difference between a man and a woman. When we marry we join ourselves to someone who is fundamentally different from us, but, mysteriously, we become one flesh with them – which means there is a total joining together, in body and spirit.

Understanding this is difficult, because it is so mysterious. But the mysterious, sacrificial, meaning of marriage is probably the main reason why there really cannot be such a thing as gay marriage.

The difference between true marriage and gay "marriage" is that when two people of the same sex join together they are embracing someone the same, rather than someone different. Doing this doesn't require the same degree of sacrifice, and it cannot involve the same degree of mystery. It cannot reflect the relationship between Jesus and his church in the way that marriage is meant to.

And because of this, and because it cannot be fruitful and is not faithful in the way described in Scripture, I do not think there can really be any such thing as gay marriage.

Is it sin to be gay?

If we say there can be no such thing as gay marriage, and that sex is only for marriage, then obviously we are saying that gay people cannot have sex.

This is going to be difficult for gay people.

The question that leads on from this is to ask, if gay people should not have sex (it would be sin if they did), is it sinful to be gay?

This is another big question! I think the simplest way to answer it is that not being married and having sexual *desires* is not necessarily sinful, but that all sexual *activity* outside marriage is wrong.

Look at it this way – if a guy sees a girl and suddenly realizes the blood is pumping round his veins at twice its normal rate, that is not a sin. It is just the natural reaction of physical attraction. It can quickly become sin though, if that attraction turns into lust, and sexual fantasy.

In a similar way, the person who finds themselves attracted to members of the same sex is not necessarily sinning. Someone who has put their hope in Christ but wrestles with homosexual temptation is no more a sinner than any other believer who has their own particular demons to face. It is what we do with those temptations and demons that counts.

Being straight and not having sex unless you are married is tough. Being gay and knowing that you can never have sex is also tough. In both cases, we need to know the Spirit, "who helps us in our weakness."[19] And we also need to know the help of our brothers and sisters in Christ – the fight against sexual sin isn't a fight we are meant to fight alone!

---

[19] Romans 8:26

Paul's Story

I grew up in a non-Christian family and made the decision to follow Christ when I was 16. I call the first 5 years of my new life the honeymoon period as things were amazing and I grew deeper and deeper in love with Jesus who had saved me from so much. However at 21 things changed.

I knew I was gay from about the age of 5. People often question me about this as 5 seems so young, but believe me, I knew that I was different and I knew I was attracted to the same sex. I had struggled for years to hide this and so when I found Jesus I thought it would all go away and for those early years things did seem to. At 21, however, through a series of events all of my own making, I had a gay affair. I met him via a phone chat line and gave myself over to sleeping with him. I was totally torn apart. I believed the bible said that being gay was the worst sin ever and so I lived in fear of being found out and thrown out of the church family I had grown to love and feel part of. I was pulled between wanting to sleep with this guy and wanting to stop.

One night I had a dream where God clearly spoke to me about being honest, he said that if I didn't own up he would make it known. Does that sound harsh? I don't think so; you see God disciplines those he LOVES that we might share in his HOLINESS. So with a lot of trepidation I arranged to meet with my lead elder. When I told him he was cool, calm and non-judgmental but I could tell underneath he was unsure what to do. He arranged to meet with the other elders, and said they would get back to me. I left the meeting feeling totally scared about what would happen next. To be honest things didn't go well and in hindsight some pastoral decisions were made that made matters worse rather than better. At one point totally out of the blue it was questioned as to whether or not I might struggle with pedophilia which I think just goes to show the lack of understanding in the church at the time about areas such as same sex attraction.

The next 5 or 6 years were incredibly painful and left me feeling alone, rejected, misunderstood and shameful. I responded to all the pain and loneliness I felt by moving from one gay encounter to the next. If I was doing well then things were ok but when I was down, depressed or hurt I would reach out to the nearest man for intimacy as sex meant I was wanted. I ended up with an eating disorder, a lot of self hate, fear of men – especially those in authority over me – and living a secret double life. I hit an all time low when I agreed to have sex for money. Prostitution had never been a plan for my life and it hit me hard that I had reached that place. So why did I live a double life? Simply because there was no way I was going to be honest to my elders again because honesty just brought more pain and pain led me to sex.

So what changed, how did I move on? That's the question people want to know when they hear about my past. Well at 27 I went to work with a ministry in Hong Kong that reaches out to prostitutes, addicts and street sleepers. What I saw there was an expression of God's grace that I had never seen before. It blew my brain to be honest and God used my time there to take me on a journey of inner healing that wasn't about simply cutting the rotten fruit off the tree of my life, coz let's face it rotten fruit just grows back. No this journey was one of finding the deeper problems that lay below the surface. I found life changing freedom from issues such as the self hate, fear, and low self worth as I allowed God to meet me in those putrid and painful places, as I took off all my masks and kicked down all my barriers of self defense. It was a journey of allowing love, grace and mercy to become real experiences and not just words. Over time I found that all the rotten fruit in my life stopped growing. After a year working amongst the disadvantaged of Hong Kong I returned to the UK a changed person. Within 2 years I met the woman who was to become my wife and we married in 2000. Four years later I became a father to the first of my 2 children. In disciplining me God has brought me through to freedom and freedom has allowed me to walk into greater levels of holiness with him. I'm no longer ashamed about my past; I live free from guilt and shame through the son of God who loves me and died for all my sins.

Chapter 4
Pornification... Or, what's so wrong with porn?

If God created bodies to be good to look at, and if he created them naked,[20] what's the problem? What harm can it do?

Porn is absolutely everywhere. We live in a visual culture and our eyes and minds are bombarded with sexual images multiple times every day. This is probably more obvious if you take a walk through Amsterdam's red light district than in some Smallesville town, but everywhere there is a TV, or a magazine rack, there is porn. In fact, there's so much of it about that we don't even notice much of the time.

This means that everyone looks at porn. Lots of people go deliberately looking for it, but no one can avoid it totally. Any mall in any town will feature advertising and shop window displays that a century ago would have been thought outrageously pornographic. Now we just think it is normal.

Does the fact that porn is normal mean it is ok then?

First off, let's be clear about what porn really is. The word *pornography* literally means "writing about prostitutes." Porn represents illicit and illegitimate sex. And it is a huge industry, which is usually at the forefront of advances in communication technology.

Back in 1953 the launch of *Playboy* magazine was revolutionary, but porn was quick to take advantage of every opportunity for expansion – from video tapes to the internet to mobile phones.

With every technological development that allowed porn to infiltrate deeper into society there has been a pushing back of the barriers of what is considered publicly acceptable. What was only worn as underwear by hookers and strippers in the 1960's has now become normal for all women,[21] and at the same time underwear

---

[20] Genesis 2:25
[21] When the first sex guide, *The Joy of Sex*, was published in 1972 it had to explain what a thong was!

(there's a clue in the name girls and boys) has become outerwear. Porn has become relentlessly harder and more transgressive. It has to. Still pictures won't cut it anymore. 'Standard' sex won't cut it anymore. Weird is now normal and there is a push for ever harder hardcore images.

This is the world you live in. It is the land of pornification.

So – what's wrong with that?

Porn is lust

The whole point of porn is to stimulate lust. Lust is what we do when we entertain sexual desire for someone we are not entitled to have sex with. Porn does this by definition – it is an image of someone you are not married to, produced in order to feed your sexual desire. In marriage sexual desire is not lust, because husband and wife are entitled to desire one another and to work out those desires sexually.

The natural conclusion of porn-stoked lust is masturbation. Porn exists to make orgasm easier. It exists to make you fake sex with someone you are not meant to have sex with.

And this is wrong.

The Bible speaks unequivocally against lust.

The Ten Commandments tell us, *You shall not commit adultery... You shall not covet your neighbors wife.*[22] Having sex with someone you are not married to – or even desiring this – is sin, and some of the Bible's most shocking imagery reflects what happens if we sell out to lust. Check out the way the prophet Ezekiel describes Israel's lustful behavior:

> At the head of every street you built your lofty place and made your beauty an abomination, offering yourself to any passerby and multiplying your whoring. You also played the whore with the Egyptians, your lustful neighbors, multiplying your whoring, to

---

[22] Exodus 20:14,17

provoke me to anger. Behold, therefore, I stretched out my hand against you and diminished your allotted portion and delivered you to the greed of your enemies, the daughters of the Philistines, who were ashamed of your lewd behavior.[23]

When she carried on her prostitution openly and exposed her nakedness, I turned away from her in disgust, just as I had turned away from her sister. Yet she became more and more promiscuous as she recalled the days of her youth, when she was a prostitute in Egypt. There she lusted after her lovers, whose genitals were like those of donkeys and whose emission was like that of horses. So you longed for the lewdness of your youth, when in Egypt your bosom was caressed and your young breasts fondled.[24]

What Ezekiel describes here is a pornified culture – a culture obsessed with sexual performance. It sounds a lot like our culture.

If you get married, having sex with your husband or wife is meant to be pure, beautiful and good. But pornified sex is like drinking from a toilet.

God speaks through the prophet Jeremiah about his people, saying, *They have forsaken me, the fountain of living waters, and hewed out cisterns for themselves, broken cisterns that can hold no water.*[25] That is exactly what happens when we use porn.

Rather than drinking toilet water, we need to develop a pure spirit, and this begins with what you look at. Even when he was in the middle of terrible suffering and distress, Job was determined to keep his spirit pure by keeping his eyes pure,

> *I made a covenant with my eyes not to look lustfully at a girl. For what is man's lot from God above, his heritage from the Almighty on high? Is it not ruin for the wicked, disaster for those who do wrong? Does he not see my ways and count my every step?*[26]

Job's attitude is a good example of Christian maturity. Being mature means having the self-control not to do some things that feel good

---

[23] Ezekiel 16:25-27
[24] Ezekiel 23:18-21
[25] Jeremiah 2:13
[26] Job 31:1-4

now because you believe that something better is coming your way *later*. This is what we call 'delayed gratification' and it runs totally against the grain of how our society teaches us to live. Our advertisement soaked world (and let's face it, porn is just another form of advertising) conditions us to want things *now*, and expect things *now*, and take things *now*. But this is not mature. It is not adult. It is what little children do – "Gimme an ice-cream, *Now!*" In contrast, someone who is mature is able to say "No" and walk on by, because he knows that there is something better waiting for him further on.

The apostle John makes this point too,

> *Do not love the world or anything in the world. If anyone loves the world, the love of the Father is not in him. For everything in the world - the cravings of sinful man, the lust of his eyes and the boasting of what he has and does - comes not from the Father but from the world. The world and its desires pass away, but the man who does the will of God lives forever.*[27]

Do you see what this passage says? The lust of the eyes (which must include looking at porn) is a sign that you are a slave to the world. It is a sign that you are not mature, but like a foolish child, because these things won't last – they will "pass away." What lasts – forever! – is what is pleasing to God.

So if you want what is going to satisfy you forever, don't blind your eyes with the passing lies of porn.

This is why Jesus warned us that it is better to gouge your eye out and enter heaven blind than to look lustfully at a woman and enter hell with your body intact.[28] If we get an adult appreciation of what is really important, really satisfying, and really lasting, we won't sell ourselves short on something that feels good now but leads to our destruction.

Grow up. Learn self-control. Learn delayed gratification. Fight lust. Don't look at porn.

---

[27] 1 John 2:15-17
[28] Matthew 5:29

How does porn work?

The book of Proverbs tells us that, *The eyes of a man are never satisfied,*[29] and the way that porn works is by captivating first the eyes, and then the rest of the senses. For someone who gets into porn, what he has already seen is never enough, because the eyes are never satisfied – there always has to be more.

It's like when you stuff yourself on a really good meal. At the end of it you will probably say something like, "I'm never going to eat another thing..." But the reality is that it will only be a few hours – at most – before you are hungry again. That's the way the appetite works, and it is how our sexual appetite works. Feed the eyes with porn, and enough is never enough. The eyes are never satisfied.

Once porn enters the eyes, it then has an effect on the rest of the body, and there is growing evidence that porn is especially powerful for men because of the way the male brain is wired.[30] Visual sexual stimulation triggers the release of hormones that hardwire the body to need more sexual stimulation. When you are married to someone, this is meant to work out well – the sight of your spouse should trigger a hormonal response that makes you desire them. But with porn it doesn't work out so well – instead creating a self-perpetuating cycle of stimulation and masturbation and the need for more stimulation.

Remember, porn exists for the purpose of masturbation. It is designed to help achieve orgasm. And orgasm is addictive because it releases dopamine – which has the same effect on the brain as heroin and cocaine. Pornographic images then get burned into the male brain by the action of noradrenaline. This is a chemical that burns memories into the brain that have physiological and emotional significance, and explains why many men have instant recall for hundreds of pornographic images. If you are married, the one body you want to be seeing in your thoughts is that of your partner.

---

[29] Proverbs 27:20
[30] For more on the science of this, see *Wired for Intimacy* by W.M. Struthers

The actions of these chemicals on the brain is to literally rewire it. A porn soaked brain becomes addicted to porn – which is why it can be so difficult to break a porn habit. It's like trying to come off crack.

All of which should make it obvious that looking at porn isn't so much about exercising your freewill, as it is about becoming a slave. Porn isn't about freedom – it leads to captivity!

Rather than becoming slaves to this trash, those of us who are followers of Jesus are called to the transformed power of a renewed mind.[31] Rather than let porn rewire our brains we are meant to develop mental pathways of holiness. We are meant to get our brains wired so that they respond to what is good, rather than to what is evil.

Porn screws up relationships

Porn is a substitute for real sex. When you look at porn you do not have to actually engage with a real person, whereas sex is meant to be all about another person. Sex that is fruitful, faithful and sacrificial is concerned about serving the person you are having sex with, and meeting their needs. Porn undermines this aspect of sex, and makes it all about you.

One of the downsides of this is that it can lead to difficulties when you do actually get into bed with someone else. If your expectation of sex is a pornified one, it makes it much more difficult to treat your sexual partner with respect and tenderness. Instead, you will probably get frustrated that they are not acting out all your porn soaked fantasies for you. Someone real, with their own needs and desires is a very different deal from the fake sex on the screen.

This is one of the reasons why so many girls think they have to act like porn stars to get and keep a guy. Which is very sad. Women shouldn't have to pretend they are porn in order to turn a guy on.

---

[31] Romans 12:2

Because of the way porn rewires the brain it can lead men to considering virtual sex to be better than real sex. As William Struthers puts it, *Porn is a whispered promise. It promises more sex, better sex, endless sex, sex on demand, more intense orgasms, experiences of transcendence. Time spent with porn prevents the user from engaging in real relationships with real people who can better meet their needs.*

This means that getting married won't stop you looking at porn. If your brain has been wired to need porn then all you will be bringing to marriage is your captivity, not true sexual freedom. Sure, you might like having sex with your wife, but she won't be enough for you. Porn will still pull you in. And this is disastrous for marriage. It leads to guilt and secrecy in men, and jealousy and insecurity in women.

So don't fall into the trap of thinking that porn is a safe sexual outlet before you get married, that you'll stop using once you are married. That's just not how it works. Instead, you need to stop using porn – *right now!*

Real sex

Let's do some theology...

Sex is immensely powerful, not only because of its physical impact on us, but because of what it offers spiritually. Sex offers us transcendence – which means something that transcends our normal experiences – something that in someway connects us to God. This is a dangerous thing to say, but it is in sex that we – in some degree – experience the closest human equivalent to the transcendent experience of union with God.

The great Christian hope is that we will be united with God. Eastern religions have mystical visions of entering nirvana, but the Christian hope is not of a vague, bodiless connection to the spiritual. Instead the Bible teaches us that we will be amazingly joined into God – spiritually *and* physically. In fact, this happens in some way as soon as we are born again. This is what Paul tells the Corinthians,

For just as the body is one and has many members, and all the members of the body, though many, are one body, so it is with Christ. For in one Spirit we were all baptized into one body – Jews or Greeks, slaves or free – and all were made to drink of one Spirit.[32]

What this incredible passage tells us is that Christians *are* the body of Christ. We are joined into him, and into one another. We are one. This is something to experience in this life, and that should shape everything we do (how can part of the body of Christ look at porn?) – but there is more to come.

The apostle John tells us that,

We are God's children now, and what we will be has not yet appeared; but we know that when he appears we shall be like him, because we shall see him as he is.[33]

This is what is called *glorification*. The day is coming when we shall see Jesus in his glory, and will share in that glory. We really are going to be like Jesus!

John then goes onto say, *And everyone who thus hopes in him* (that's Jesus) *purifies himself* (that's you and me) *as he* (Jesus) *is pure.[34]*

Do you see how this connects together? If you are a Christian you are already joined into Christ, but one day this is going to become overwhelmingly real. So, because of this, the only appropriate way to live now is with a Christ-like purity.

So how does this make sex transcendent?

Here's the deal – our union with Christ is indescribable. It really is a "you had to be there" experience. Being united with God is something that really shouldn't be possible, but that God in his grace makes possible. And sex is like a reflection of this.

---

[32] 1 Corinthians 12:12-13
[33] 1 John 3:2
[34] 1 John 3:3

When you have sex with someone you enter into a degree of unity with them that shouldn't be possible. No two people should be able to get that close – but sex makes it possible. When this happens in marriage it is beautiful and pure and good. It is a reflection of our union with Christ that God blesses and smiles on. But when it happens outside of marriage that reflection is horribly smashed up. Which is why Paul warns the Corinthians,

> *Do you not know that your bodies are members of Christ? Shall I then take the members of Christ and make them members of a prostitute? Never! Or do you not know that he who is joined to a prostitute becomes one body with her? For, as it is written, "The two will become one flesh."[35]*

Having sex with someone you are not meant to doesn't stop you from becoming "one" with them – it just means that oneness is terribly, horribly wrong.

So what porn does, is apparently offer you the transcendence of sex, but in a way that totally corrupts what real sex is designed to achieve.

It stinks.

Pure sex

The abuse of sex – including using porn – inevitably messes up our relationship with God, and with other people. It shatters what is meant to be transcendent and turns it into a sewer. Look at it this way – having water in your house is very important. There are pipes which water is meant to flow out of, and other pipes down which it is meant to flow away. And as long as water is in the right pipes at the right time it is fantastic – water for washing, drinking, and flushing the toilet. But if rather than filling a sink, water is left running over the floor, or if rather than going down the sewer, dirty water backs up in the bath, it is horrible and destructive.

---

[35] 1 Corinthians 6:15-16

That's what sex outside marriage is like, and it is what porn is like. Porn is like a leaking toilet that fills a house with the stench of excrement.

The Bible tells men to, *Treat older women like mothers, younger women like sisters, in all purity.*[36] Women are not just plumbing! They are beautiful creations of God and are to be honored and respected, not someone to just dump your biological waste into! Unless you are very sick you would not want to masturbate over pictures of your mother or sister – well, men, you should treat all women like your mother or sister.

The Bible tells us that, *Man is the image and glory of God, and woman is the glory of man.*[37] We should act in a way that reflects this – and there is nothing glorious about looking at porn.

So we are to do things that are beneficial for us[38] and regard sexual purity with the utmost seriousness. This means treating sexual sin with radical decisiveness, rather than allowing it to stink up the house of our lives.

Girls on porn

Most of this chapter has been directed towards the boys, because porn is a particular problem for men – but that doesn't mean that porn has no impact on girls. An increasing number of women seem to be using porn in a similar way to how men do, and this is just as wrong. Also, there is the very practical question of how girls should respond to boys who are into porn.

One of the most important things a girl can do is refuse to act in the way a pornified culture expects. Don't send your boyfriend a sexy picture of you to put on his phone. You are not a sex object, so don't act like one. And letting those kind of pictures get out there is just madness – do you really want all his friends looking at a picture of you naked? Be wise about what pictures you put up on Facebook. Once a picture is up on the internet it is impossible to delete it.

---

[36] 1 Timothy 5:2
[37] 1 Corinthians 11:7
[38] 1 Corinthians 10:23

If a boy wants you to act like a porn star in the way that you dress, talk or act, just walk away. He isn't worth it.

Another area which girls (more than boys) need to watch out for is getting fixated on romance. This might be books you read, or movies you watch, but if you find yourself constantly daydreaming about some romantic story or character your brain is going to turn to mush. It doesn't make much difference whether you are Team Edward or Team Jacob – spending all your time fantasizing about them is not going to help your relationship with Jesus!

Don't sell yourself short. Don't fall for the lies of pornification.

Chapter 5
Living in a divorce culture... Or, what happens when nothing lasts?

When I was growing up (which isn't *that* long ago) divorce was rare. Most of the kids in my class at school had both their parents at home, and their parents were married. That has all changed now, and divorce is normal.

When something is normal we tend to take it for granted. We also tend not to question it. But divorce isn't something we should ever take for granted, or fail to question. We ought to look it square in the face, and be honest about its impact upon us all.

And divorce does affect us all – even someone like me, who grew up when divorce was rare, and has never been divorced, and whose parents are still together after 40+ years of marriage.

Our culture teaches sexual liberation but this actually results in a lot of screw ups. At the deep end we see sexual abuse, rape, AIDS, abortion, and so on, but everyone is affected by the divorce statistics. Broken hearts are all around us, and that affects us all. For one thing, it just makes life messy and complicated. It is messy for the kids of divorcees who spend every weekend being bussed from one set of parents to the next. And it is messy for divorcees who have to spend every weekend shuttling their kids backwards and forwards with ex-partners. It creates mess in families and it creates complexity in neighborhoods – is that the same guy who was living there last month, or has she got another boyfriend? Quite often the children in these families end up having to act more like responsible adults than their parents do, and that's not right.

Living in a divorce culture means that trying to work out sexuality and relationships is confusing, in a way it wasn't for previous generations. It used to be the case that life was pretty clearly marked out for most people. You would go to school, leave school, get a job, get married to someone your parents approved of, settle down, have kids – and then watch the cycle repeat itself. For some people this predictability looked terrifyingly restricting and boring, but it did have the advantage of keeping things simple. Life now is complicated! How are you supposed to know who to marry, or even whether to marry? How many people do you need to sleep with before finding the one who you want to sleep with long term? And how long term is long term going to be anyway, when so many relationships fall apart?

All of us are affected by our cultural expectation that relationships don't last. My kids are affected by it, even though their parents and grandparents have never got divorced. They just swallow it up from their culture. This is the culture in which you swim, and it has affected you.

There are some serious consequences to this. One is fear. I meet lots of fearful people – people who are afraid that if they commit to anything they will get dumped and hurt; people who fear to make a commitment in case a better option later comes along; people who fear they will never taste true love. And I meet plenty of people who try to overcome these fears by grabbing hold of any relationship they can in order to boost their sense of self-worth, only to be taken advantage of and screwed up.

One of the most heartbreaking things I have experienced as a pastor is seeing someone come to faith in Jesus, start to do well and become a disciple, only to throw it all away because of a sexual relationship.

If we are to break the power of divorce over our lives we need to understand some fundamental things about the nature of God. We need to understand that he is our *Father*, who is *faithful*, and that he is our *redeemer*.

God the Father

Jesus taught his disciples to pray "Our Father."[39]

That we get to call God *Father* is one of the greatest privileges of being a Christian, but it is also something that many people struggle with because of their relationship with their own father.

---

[39] Matthew 6:9

Most people have some kind of issue with their dad, because no earthly father is perfect – and some fathers are just horrible.

I have spent hours and hours talking with people trying to get them to understand what it means to call God "Father" – all the time having to peel back the layers of hurt and confusion caused by earthly fathers. If you are one of those people who even finds the word *father* painful, don't give up. Press into this and ask God to show you what a real father is like.

The fact that God has decided we should know him as Father must mean that there are things we are meant to understand about him based on our understanding of our human fathers. Whenever we see a father doing what fathers are meant to do, that gives us a picture of what God is like. However, our experience of our fathers will never map exactly with what God our Father is really like – even if our fathers are fantastic!

I like to think I'm a pretty good dad to my kids. I tell them I love them (and I really do love them!). I take time to play with them. I'm interested in how they are doing at school. I provide them with security and make sure they have food to eat and clothes to wear. I like to give them treats. I don't beat them or abuse them. But even if I get these things right, there is plenty that I get wrong. There are times when I am impatient, or tired and grumpy. There are times when I don't listen properly and understand what they need me to know. There are times when I'm more interested in what I'm interested in than in the things they want me to show interest in. There are times when I make the wrong judgment calls and do not act with complete fairness. So my fathering is a mixture of the good and the not so good – and that is inevitable because I am a human!

Some other dads do a better job of fathering than I do. Sadly, many do a lot worse. But even at their best, human dads only point to what God our Father is like; and human dads at their worst totally undermine what we are meant to understand about our heavenly Father.

I think of the woman I spoke to who had suffered terrible abuse at the hands of her father. He abused her sexually, didn't give her enough food to eat and treated her in ways too shameful to talk about. For her to come to a place where she felt secure in the love of a heavenly Father who is so radically different from her earthly father was a long and tortuous journey.

But here's the thing: The Bible makes it clear that Jesus came to make the Father known to us. We are meant to know God as the Father he really is, not as we might imagine him to be – and the way that we do this is by Jesus. If you want to know what God the Father is like, you need look no further than God the Son. Jesus made this clear to his disciples on the night of his betrayal. He told them, "Whoever has seen me has seen the Father."[40] So if you wonder what the Father is like, look at Jesus!

When we look at Jesus we see someone who is amazingly tender and kind. He was incredibly patient with people that everyone else had rejected. He was happy to have little kids come and jump on him. He had incredible compassion for the sick and distressed. We also see Jesus as someone who was tough. He didn't shy from confrontation, and didn't keep his mouth shut when something needed to be said. He had amazing authority, and could do impossible things like make storms stop. And he was awesomely brave. He looked torture and death in the face and didn't turn from it.

All this makes Jesus a very attractive person – it makes him someone we would all want to spend time with. And all that attracts us to Jesus is also what should attract us to his Father, because Father and Son are just like one another.

Jesus also explained that the reason he was making the Father known to his disciples was so that we might know the love with which the Father loves Jesus.[41] The Father and Son have overwhelming love for one another – and they want you to share in this.

Grasping this is to plunge yourself into deep Trinitarian waters: God is one, but God is also three. The Father loves the Son; the Son came to earth to make the Father's love known to his people; and

---

[40] John 14:9
[41] John 17:24-26

now the Spirit is the one who works in our hearts and enables us to cry out to God, "Abba! Father!"[42]

If we can get our heads around what it means to have a Father in heaven who is like this, it will transform our attitude towards relationships. If you know that God is your Father and is crazy-passionately in love with you, it's going to change how you look at the world. It will bring you into such a place of security that you won't need to trash yourself by getting into sexual relationships that do you no good. And it will give you the confidence and security to think about marriage positively rather than fearfully – because if God loves you like he does, he must be able to make it possible for you and your marriage partner to love each other in a similar way – a way that goes beyond any of your past experiences.

God is Father! We don't have to have to let a divorce culture have the last word.

God is Faithful

God is faithful!

Man, it is hard to grasp what this means coming from where we come from. We looked at faithfulness in Chapter 2, but it is such an important subject it's worth us looking at it again quickly...

We just don't do faithfulness anymore. We might say 'BFF' but we know that nothing really lasts forever. Living in a divorce culture has trained us to think of faithfulness as being something that is temporary at best. This is why people talk about being 'serial monogamists' – they are faithful to the person they are sleeping with, but only for a while, before they move onto someone else's bed.

This is not how things should be.

To try and understand what faithfulness is really about we must understand that God is not relative but absolute. What this means

---

[42] Romans 8:15

is that God doesn't change. The reason our human relationships so often fall apart rather than stay faithful is because we are so changeable. How we feel about someone changes and we decide we don't want to be with them anymore. We say things like, "I did love you, but things change, and I need to move on."

But God never moves on.

God's love is absolute. It doesn't change. When God has declared his faithfulness to someone, that never shifts. The book of James tells us that in our heavenly Father there is "no variation or shadow due to change."[43]

God is faithful!

We see the faithfulness of God worked out in the life of Jesus. The book of Hebrews tells us that Jesus was *faithful* to his Father, and that he is *faithful* over God's house.[44] Being faithful over God's house means that Jesus is faithfully watching over all his Father's people and will not let them go. Jesus isn't going to trash the house!

Because faithfulness is so central to the character of God it shapes his every action – and we need to learn to let it shape ours, too. Faithfulness is the antidote to our divorce culture because where there is faithfulness there is no divorce. So we need to let the faithfulness of God get deep into our hearts and transform us into people who are faithful too – faithful to our friends, our communities, our churches, to the person we marry, and to God himself.

If you want to be a world changer, learn to be faithful – it's what's going to break the power of divorce.

---

[43] James 1:17
[44] Hebrews 3:2-6

Jesus is our Redeemer

The book of Hebrews tells us that Jesus has secured "eternal redemption" for his people by his death on the cross.[45] To be redeemed means to be rescued, saved and delivered. It means that once we turn to Jesus, Satan no longer has any authority over us. We are free!

By freeing us in this way Jesus redeems us from the power of guilt and shame. To see what this means it is helpful for us to use two theological words: *Propitiation* and *expiation*. Don't worry if these words sound complicated – they are going to help you!

Many people live with a deep sense of shame. Shame is something we experience when we feel an outcast from our social group. It is often caused by sin that has been committed *against* you. For instance, those who have been sexually abused often feel shame – a sense they are dirty and worthless, that they are like modern day lepers. Shame sucks in power from a divorce culture. The reality of shattered relationships leaves many of us with a deep sense that we will never find relationships where we are simply accepted as we are – but that instead we will face constant rejection.

The way that shame gets crucified is to lay hold of the death of Christ which is our *expiation*. This means that Christ's death has absorbed all the sin that has defiled us. Christ's death means you are no longer defiled by what others have done to you, but declared spotless because of Christ's atoning blood.

Laying hold of this also means developing the practice of forgiveness. As long as we remain in unforgiveness to someone, we are not free from what they have done to us. In a divorce culture there are probably many people who have done many things to you that should not have been done. The only way to escape the shame and bitterness of this is to come to the cross and let Jesus be your expiation – because at the cross he has redeemed you.

As well as shame, we also need to know redemption from our guilt. Guilt is what we feel when we know we have done something we

---

[45] Hebrews 9:11-14

should not have done. Guilt is the consequence of sin committed *by* you. Guilt is objective: Each of us is guilty! None of us has lived to a standard that is acceptable according to God's perfect standard. This means that we all deserve God's anger and judgment.

This is a desperate place to be!

Guilt also sucks up power from our divorce culture, because our culture leads us all into sin. Our culture encourages us to think selfishly and to act faithlessly. All of us end up letting other people down and failing to keep our commitments and the power of guilt thrives on this!

The only way out of this mess is to lay hold of the death of Christ which is our *propitiation*. This means that the wrath of God which should be our just reward has instead been carried by Christ. God's anger has been turned away from us and poured out on Jesus instead. It was this awesome sacrificial act that guarantees our eternal redemption.

Amazing!

Once we get hold of what it means to be redeemed we will be able to look at life with new freedom and confidence. Rather than letting our culture drag us down, the cross of Christ will raise us up! Get hold of this, and of the fact that God is faithful, and your heavenly father, and you will begin to walk free!

Sue's Story

My story is that of redemption from a destructive sexual past. It is a story of restoration!

It is the kindness and goodness of God that leads us to repentance, not the big stick! Our sin separates us from him and that's why God hates it. He wants to restore you in order to restore intimacy. He wants to restore you because he has a far, far better way to meet your need for intimacy than the one you are caught up in.

This life we lead with him and this story he has caught us up into is HIS story and it's the greatest love affair in all of history. It is the love of the Father that sent the Son and He did it because He wanted you; He wanted an intimate, personal love affair with you!

The Bible is littered with stories that illustrate this.

For example, the prophet Hosea was ordered to marry an adulterous wife and to take her back when she was unfaithful to him. Hosea was told to keep loving her because God wanted a graphic illustration of his relationship with the Israelites and how He felt when they abandoned Him for idols. The Israelites were disloyal to God because they worshipped other gods as the source of abundance and life. They did not trust God to meet their needs.

So what's my story and how does it relate to what I am saying?

I got married at age 25 and after 3 years my husband left me and I got divorced at age 30. I was left feeling like damaged goods. I was reeling and in a state of shame and shock. This led me into 3 relationships one after another, all lasting several years and all of which became sexual.

How and why? Why, as a mature Christian of 15 years would I take up this kind of lifestyle – why?

Because I had unresolved issues and questions around my identity. My father was emotionally absent and never told me he loved me or that I was beautiful. I didn't know who I was or whether I was loveable or not. I was hungry for love, for touch and for affirmation and I found that being desired by a man was a powerful drug to me.

Sexual sin is about comfort and identity and when I found a form of love and affirmation in sex it became idolatrous because – as the Israelites did – I gave my heart, time and affection to it and my behavior revealed the lack of trust in my heart. I did not believe that God could or would meet my deep need for intimacy. Or if I did, I wasn't prepared to wait!

We crave intimacy; we are built for it. We desire to be intimate with the opposite sex; God has made it that way. However, sex is a powerful and deep connection between two people, ultimately an expression of love and commitment. Marriage (in which sex plays a big part) is meant to reflect the deep level of intimacy and union that God desires with his bride, us, the church. Where we become knitted in to Him and all that we need is found in Him.

The bonds that are created when we have sex are powerful and they tie you in and create a connection that is EXTREMELY difficult to break away from. We are spiritual and physical beings and when we have sex with a person it connects us with them in ways that are mysterious and unseen. Once you have had sex with someone your soul becomes tied into them and it will confuse you and muddy your ability to work out if you are compatible or not. Sex becomes a focus in a relationship and you will feel like you are being intimate; however, it is quite possible to have sex and give your body intimately but withhold your heart and soul. If you are not committing to marry someone then I can guarantee you will most likely be giving of your body more than your heart – especially if you feel you are unlovable! It will be a trade off for you as it was for me; giving your body in order to have your deeper heart's cry met.

These soul ties that are created are devastating to break; I know this from personal experience. Each of the relationships I had that were sexual took enormous strength to walk away from as it felt like I was walking away from that which was giving me life. I could only do it because I knew that God offered something better. In Jeremiah God says of the Israelites:

"My people have committed two sins:
They have forsaken me,
  the spring of living water,
and have dug their own cisterns,
  broken cisterns that cannot hold water"

I was attempting to get my needs met from a filthy, cracked, broken source instead of coming to God – the spring of living water – and I wanted to be free!

Remember you will reap what you sow! I know this! I felt like my heart and soul were tearing from me each time I got into and out of a relationship and it was slowly destroying me as I would repeatedly come up against my inability to forgive myself each time I went back. I felt that I was losing all that was beautiful in me; all that reflected who Jesus was in my life.

When we sin sexually, as 1 Corinthians says, we sin against our own bodies and it devastates us to the core and to the center of our hearts and it is a form of self-harm. During my time of recovery and coming out of these relationships, Psalm 51 became the Psalm of my life: "Against you and you only have I sinned and done what is evil in your sight...cleanse me and I shall be clean... wash me whiter than snow...create in me a pure heart... restore to me the joy of my salvation."

I once felt like "damaged goods" but that is not the truth and Isaiah 61 says God removes your shame and gives you instead a double portion and everlasting joy will be yours.

My testimony is that there is nothing and no-one who compares to Jesus. There is no intimacy that is deeper or more powerful than that which we have with him. I know, because I have had both. One leads to death and one leads to life. Intimacy with Him is true freedom from the bondage of sexual sin.

Question Time...

Q. Is it a sin to masturbate?

OK lets clear this one up – pretty much everyone masturbates, but there are some people who do not. I remember once having a very funny conversation in a car with a bunch of leaders from my church. One of them said, "I have never masturbated" while another said, "I can honestly put my hand on my heart and say that before getting married there was never a day that went by…"

Also, this is not just a guy thing – girls masturbate too.

So if most people do it, does that make it ok?

Christians have often got themselves tied in knots over this subject. Masturbation has been viewed as an appalling vice, with dire consequences, like making you go blind. (It doesn't – there would be a lot more blind people around if it did!) But then other people have been very relaxed about it, saying it is of no consequence whatsoever.

What should we think?

The reason that masturbation is often viewed as sinful is that it is said that it is always accompanied by lustful thoughts. We know lust is wrong, so masturbation must be wrong. Simple.

But the thing is that this isn't quite true, and I just don't think it is helpful when people say things like, "Masturbation is always wrong because it is always a response to lust." Certainly for guys (who I know more about, for obvious reasons) masturbating can at times be little different from sneezing – just a physical thing with no thought involved at all! When masturbating is like this, it is difficult for me to see it as being much of a problem. (Although some guys tell me that for them lust is *always* involved with masturbation – which means it will always be wrong.)

There is a practical consideration though – if a guy gets into the habit of masturbating and coming to orgasm very quickly (like sneezing), he is actually training his body for premature ejaculation. Once you are married your wife will not appreciate it if you have an orgasm before she has even finished getting undressed! She will need you to demonstrate some self-control. So, to prevent this, you might try masturbating slowly – but try doing that without your mind wandering to lustful thoughts... I'm not sure that's possible.

The reality is that much of the time masturbating *is* done in response to lustful thoughts, and this is wrong. The thing to focus on though, is your *thoughts*, more than the masturbating itself. It is your thoughts that are the problem. Get them sorted out and the other stuff will sort itself out. There is also the reality that it is often porn that is feeding masturbation – in a sense porn exists in order to facilitate masturbation. So if porn is your reason for masturbating, then porn is your problem.

Something people often ask is, "What about using masturbation as a release valve? Isn't it better to quickly rub one out and relieve the pressure, which can then stop you from having sexual fantasies?" I read one book that said guys shouldn't do this but wait for a wet dream, which is God's provision to men so they don't need to masturbate. To be honest, this seems crazy to me! Wet dreams happen when you dream about sex, so how is that a good thing if your dream is lustful, and you spend the whole of the next day reliving it?!

Masturbation is like sex, but sex with everyone and no-one at the same time. While masturbating you can fantasize about having sex with any number of people, but the only person actually in the room is you. This is not how God designed sex to be. Sex is meant to be an activity enjoyed by a man and a woman together. Getting into the habit of the sexless sex of masturbation can make it more difficult for us to relate to members of the opposite sex as we should. It can make us look at other people lustfully – basically as mind-fuel for our masturbating. And if we do get married it can mean we have trained ourselves to view sex selfishly, or lazily – as something that is just about getting what we want, rather than something by which we are meant to bless someone else.

Another problem with masturbation is the sense of guilt it can produce. If a young guy is trying to faithfully follow Jesus but is also masturbating every day it is easy to get trapped in a cycle of guilt, and for this to have a very negative impact on his relationship with God. We are not meant to walk in guilt but in freedom.

So the real problems with masturbation are if it is being fuelled by lust or porn, and if it is trapping you in guilt. The thing we need to do is focus on the heart, and get that right first. Without the heart being changed, our thoughts, and our behavior, will never change.

Jesus said, "Everyone who looks at a woman with lustful intent has already committed adultery with her in his heart. If your right eye causes you to sin, tear it out and throw it away. For it is better that you lose one of your members than that your whole body be thrown into hell."[46] You see what the problem is here? It's a sinful heart. We have to win the battle in our hearts, which means we become more concerned with pleasing Jesus than we are with the things that sin offers us. We can also see that Jesus takes this seriously – adultery is so terrible it would be better to stick a knife in your eye than to even think of having sex with someone you're not married to.

But we can't do this on our own. We need help! And help is available. Our most important helper is the Holy Spirit. Jesus promised that he would send the Spirit to help us.[47] Another way of translating the word 'Helper' is 'Comforter' or 'Fortifier'. The Spirit is one who helps us fight sin, he offers us greater comfort than sin offers, and he fortifies us so we can resist temptation.

When we are tempted – especially sexually – it is a great help to pray for the assistance of the Holy Spirit. This is like being able to get on the phone to a superhero and have him instantly available to save you! When tempted, pray a simple prayer – "Holy Spirit, Jesus promised you would be a Helper, a Comforter, a Fortifier for his people. Now would you help me in this situation. Would you comfort me. Would you make me strong." Then take a deep breath, count to three, and let God keep his promise. I find again and again that doing this gets me out of trouble!

As well as the help of the Holy Spirit, God has given us the church to help us. Each of us needs to be part of a congregation where there

---

[46] Matthew 5:28-29
[47] John 14:26

are other faithful followers of Christ who can help us. Talk with someone, make yourself accountable to someone – don't try and fight this battle on your own.

And when you do sin, when your heart is lustful, or if you get stuck in a habit of masturbating that is trapping you in guilt – confess! It is good to confess to God, so he can forgive us, and to other people, so that they can help us. God promises us, "If we confess our sins, he is faithful and just to forgive us our sins and to cleanse us from all unrighteousness."[48]

---

[48] 1 John 1:9

Q. How do you know if you're attracted to someone if you cannot make love with them? What if they are rubbish in bed!?

This is a question lots of people ask, but it's a weird one! It reflects our pornified culture rather than a biblical understanding of love and marriage. It reflects the kind of attitude that the prophet Ezekiel describes the people of Judah as having – an obsession with men being hung like donkeys and having five-times-a-night staying power.[49]

It also reflects a culture where we treat everything – and everybody – as disposable. We get bored quickly, chuck what we have in to landfill, and get a new version. Lots of people treat relationships like this, but it is not what followers of Jesus are to do.

And anyway, if you are going to make performance in the bedroom the chief criterion for deciding who to marry, how will you ever know you will find the right person? How many partners will you have to test out to ensure that the one you finally settle for is up to scratch? And what if you ditch one person and go onto another but then realize that the first person was better in bed than the latest one – what are you going to do then?!

This is no way to decide on a relationship.

If you are thinking about someone to marry there are a number of much more important things you should look for. These are the kind of questions I would want to ask:[50]

Is there evidence of God's call on your relationship? The most important and basic question that can be asked before deciding to marry is, "Am I called to love this person with a lifetimes sacrificial love?"[51] Unless you can answer this question positively there is not much point in pursuing the relationship to marriage.

Does the inner witness of the Holy Spirit confirm your relationship? Do you have a sense that God is joining you together?

---

[49] See Ezekiel 23
[50] Thanks to PJ Smyth for help with this section
[51] Ephesians 5:22-33

Are you both believers?[52] In the Old Testament God commanded his people that they were not to plow with an ox and a donkey yoked together.[53] This was an example of legislation to prevent cruelty to animals. As an ox and a donkey have different strength and work at different speeds, to yoke them together would cause one of them distress. When a believer marries an unbeliever distress inevitably enters the relationship. Your fundamental desires and priorities in life will be different and the unbeliever will not be able to encourage the believer in their spiritual growth. What might look attractive now will actually result in cruelty later on.

Sometimes believers begin relationships with unbelievers in the hope that they will become Christians. While it is true that by God's grace this does sometimes happen, I have seen far more examples of such an approach ultimately destroying the believers relationship with Jesus. Don't do it!

The Bible tells us that "Charm is deceitful, and beauty is vain, but a woman who fears the Lord is to be praised."[54] So you are making a much better choice for the long term if you find someone who loves Jesus, than simply someone who promises you a good time in the sack.

Is the whole situation in line with God's word? For example, you cannot already be married; nor is a gay marriage permissible.

Is there evidence of mutual benefit? Does your relationship do you good? Does it make you happy or miserable? Has it helped or hindered your relationship with Jesus? Do other people benefit from your relationship, e.g., has your circle of friends enlarged or decreased since you have been together?

Are you both ready to leave and cleave?[55] The Order of Service we use at weddings at my church states this:

> *The Scripture tells us that Christ loved His church and gave Himself up for her. This same attitude of unselfish care is to be the character of*

---

[52] 2 Corinthians 6:14
[53] Deuteronomy 22:10
[54] Proverbs 31:30
[55] Genesis 2:24

their new life together. When Adam said of his wife "this is now bone of my bones and flesh of my flesh", God replied saying: "For this reason a man will leave his father and mother and be united to his wife, and they will become one flesh".

From this we understand that marriage is a separation from parental authority. God expects X and Y to be responsible to and for one another from this day on. They are entering a union, joined by God, which Scripture says is "honorable". Therefore they enter it joyfully and reverently, looking to the Lord for grace and help.

In order to enter such a relationship you need to be at a marriageable place in terms of maturity and finances.

Have you seen each other's inner character? Dating is trial and error. Dating is about hiding the real me behind make-up and dancing. Courtship is about testing one another's character and the rightness of the relationship before God and man.

Do your team of advisors confirm the relationship? This would usually include parents, trusted friends and church leaders.

Does common sense confirm your relationship? Are you compatible? Are you financially viable? Are you happy with each others career path projections?

If you can work through all these questions positively you won't need to worry too much about whether you are going to enjoy sex with one another – don't worry, you're going to love it!

Q. Is it wrong to date a lesbian while she is dating another girl?

I assume this was a question asked by a guy rather than a girl. Either way the answer is easy: Yes, it would be wrong!

Q. What are the boundaries of sex within marriage? Is anal sex okay in marriage?

The question about anal sex is an interesting one. Up to a few years ago this is something that had never even crossed my mind – in my simple way of thinking vaginas were made for sex, and anuses for crapping. But it is a question that seems to be asked more and more. Why is this? My hunch is that it is a result of our pornified culture, as porn (so I'm told) often features anal sex.

The thing about porn is that it fails to represent sex as sex is meant to be. The soft porn in the magazines of my teenage years featured naked women lying in provocative poses, but the ever harder porn of the internet age features ever more bizarre sexual activity – it has to, because those who use it need ever more graphic images to get the same high, just like an alcoholic has to consume ever increasing amounts of booze. Pornified sex is abusive, transgressive and voyeuristic. It does not represent the faithful love of one man and one woman but the use of men and women as plumbing.

In pornified sex, every orifice is simply somewhere to fit a penis.

The boundaries for sex within marriage are the same for the boundaries for sex outside of marriage – What honors Jesus and blesses other people? Basically this means you can do anything that you want, so long as you can do it with a clear conscience and your spouse can do it with a clear conscience – and with enjoyment. The book of Hebrews tells us to "let the marriage bed be undefiled"[56] which means we shouldn't do anything in bed that dishonors God or our marriage partner.

It is important though that your conscience is educated by the Bible and by the Spirit of God, rather than by your culture. If you have used porn, or even if you have grown up watching fairly run of the mill mainstream movies (or Lady Gaga videos), your brain will carry all kinds of sexual imagery which is shaped by a sinful culture rather than by the Bible.

---

[56] Hebrews 13:4

The book of the Bible that describes most explicitly sexual love is the Song of Songs. This book is very erotic, and in poetic language describes very intimate things, including oral sex. It does all this, however, in the context of a relationship between one man and one woman. It is a relationship sanctified by marriage, and it is beautiful, not sordid.

The Song of Songs describes some of the things that godly lovers can do, but it doesn't set out a list of approved and banned sexual practices! The Bible doesn't tend to work that way. The way it works is to get our hearts lined up with God, so that our thoughts and actions then bring pleasure to him.

To get back to the question of anal sex then, it is really more a question of the heart than of the orifice. Some Christians would argue that it is totally acceptable. If both husband and wife are turned on by it, what's the problem? Maybe this is right, but I'm not so sure it is – I think it is a pornified thing to do, and I think anuses are for crapping, not sex. There is also the medical reality that anal sex is potentially risky. The anus can easily tear and bleed, which can lead to infection, and anal sex can damage the sphincter muscles, leading to problems with incontinence – and that doesn't sound much fun to me...

Q. Is oral sex or masturbating each other ok before marriage if you're in a serious relationship? How would you know what the limits are, like whether kissing is too far or feeling is too far?

There was once a President of the USA called Bill Clinton who was accused of having an affair with a young assistant called Monica Lewinsky. Clinton denied this categorically, making a famous televised speech in which he tearfully stated, "I did not have sexual relations with that woman."

Turned out she'd been giving him blow jobs in the oval office.

Because our hearts are deceitful, and our culture is sexually warped, there is a way of thinking that considers an activity to be 'sex' only if it involves a penis entering a vagina. But this is like saying you're only drinking coffee if it is an espresso. Dude, there may be a lot of milk and chocolate in that mocha, but it's still coffee! My point is this: If you are bringing one another to orgasm you are having sex. And even if you are not getting to orgasm, if you are sexually intimate, it is sex.

So no, oral sex or masturbating are not ok before marriage. Wake up and smell the coffee.

The trouble with all questions asking about what the limits should be before marriage is that it is the wrong question! As followers of Jesus we shouldn't be trying to push the limits as far as we can but to become as Christ-like as we can. Asking what the limits are is really the wrong question. The right question to ask is, "What is going to most help me to worship Jesus in this situation?"

The Song of Songs warns us not to awaken or arouse love until the right time. In practical terms what this means is that we should not be getting into situations where our physical and emotional passions for someone else are being aroused in a way which is not appropriate outside of marriage. And this probably means that you need to pull the line way back. I have some friends who didn't even kiss each other until they were married. That may seem plain weird, but it must have been amazing. It was also very wise. Speaking from experience, it is very difficult to have a serious kiss with someone and not get sexually stimulated. Sometimes it doesn't even take a serious kiss...

So the line is simply this: Don't do anything that gets you too hot and horny. Save it for your marriage.

Another helpful rule of thumb is the Apostle Paul's instruction to his disciple Timothy to "treat younger women like sisters, and older women like mothers."[57] What this means (and I'm speaking to the guys here, but the principle holds good the other way around) is you should treat any woman you are not married to like a sister or mother – and unless there is something seriously wrong with you, you wouldn't want to touch up your sister or mother...

---

[57] 1 Timothy 5:2

Q. How does a Christian cope with being accused of homophobia if you take a Biblical stance on homosexuality?

One of the things we should expect as Christians is to be abused and misrepresented. Jesus himself said, "Blessed are you when others revile you and persecute you and utter all kinds of evil against you on my account."[58]

So if someone gives you a hard time for what you believe, just take it on the chin. Welcome to normal Christian life!

But when it comes to the question of homosexuality the key thing is that there is no truth in the accusation that we are homophobic. Our heart attitude towards other people needs to be one of love and compassion. If this reflects what we really are, then people will see that we don't have phobias about anyone – we still might get slandered, but most people will know that the accusation has no basis in reality.

---

[58] Matthew 5:11

Q. How do you help/react to a gay Christian friend who is struggling and shutting herself off from church?

The same way that you would respond to a straight friend who is struggling or shutting themselves off from church! Someone's sexual orientation isn't really the issue – what counts is their relationship with Jesus and his people.

The Apostle Paul gives us some great advice in his first letter to the Thessalonians. He tells us to, 'admonish the idle, encourage the fainthearted, help the weak, be patient with them all.'[59] So if someone is struggling the thing we need to work out is whether they are struggling because they are lazy, because they are depressed, or because they are weak – and we should then respond in the appropriate way.

---

[59] 1 Thessalonians 5:14

Q. I have lots of gay friends. What's the best way to share the gospel with them?

The same way you would with anyone! The issue is not that they are gay, but that they are sinners who need to experience the grace of God – just like everyone else. So the thing to think about is how the story of God's grace will best connect with them.

Think about the example of Paul in Philippi and the different people who came to faith there.[60] The businesswoman Lydia needed to be convinced of the reality that Jesus is the one way to God. The demon possessed girl needed to have the strongholds in her life broken. The jailer needed a demonstration of the power of God. Each of these people was different, and needed to see the reality of God in a different way, but for each of them the key thing was that they encountered Jesus.

The same is true with your friends.

---

[60] See Acts 16:11-40

Q. Were there any gay people in the Bible?

No-one is described as 'gay' in the Bible, but then the concept of being gay is only a very recent idea. Homosexuality is described, but always in a negative way. So we know that there were people in biblical times who had homosexual sex, and this is something that the Bible never approves.

Were there people in Israel or in the early church who had same sex attraction? Probably. But the Bible never describes this – certainly not as a legitimate lifestyle choice.

Some gay Christians try to claim that David and Jonathan were gay, but there is no evidence for this. What we know about David is that it was his attraction to women that got him into trouble, not any attraction to men.

Q. What about gay churches?

There are an increasing number of gay churches. These churches form as places where gay people can go without feeling they have to apologize for who they are, and where others will understand and accept them. Gay churches also exist as places where gay people can work out there sexual desires and claim to be followers of Jesus, and not have anyone tell them that this is hypocritical or inconsistent.

Ultimately, how you view this comes down to your understanding of scripture. If your understanding (the correct understanding) is that all sex outside marriage (real, heterosexual marriage of course) is wrong, then there is no place for a church that teaches people they can have sex in any other context. Such a church is in serious error and sin.

Church should be a place where all kinds of people are welcome and where together all these different people find the grace of God to live in a way that is pleasing to Jesus. If churches function this way then there is no need for a gay church. For me, church functions best when it contains a cross section of society – old and young, rich and poor, different ethnicities, different histories. I believe this is what the Bible teaches us church should be like. Gay people should be welcome in this kind of church and, like the rest of us, in church find a place to glorify God and serve other people.

Q. So do people not have sex in heaven? And if not, why not?

Jesus was once asked a question about marriage in the resurrection – the world as it will be once God has renewed the heavens and the earth. (It is more helpful to think about life in the new heavens and earth than to talk about 'heaven' as it is the new heavens and earth which we are ultimately going to live in.) Jesus' response was, 'in the resurrection they neither marry not are given in marriage, but are like the angels in heaven.'[61]

The biblical expectation of sex is that it is something that should only take place within the covenant relationship of marriage. So if there is no marriage in the resurrection it seems there will be no sex either.

This might sound like very bad news! It is the kind of news that means many young people hope that Jesus doesn't return until they've had the opportunity to lose their virginity!

And why would there be no sex in the resurrection? If sex is so good, why won't it continue forever?

I think the answer is found in the things that sex is meant to achieve. One of those things is the creation of new life – sex is meant to result in babies! But in the resurrection there will be no need for further reproduction. The new heavens and earth will be filled with God's people and the creation command to Adam and Eve to be fruitful and multiply will no longer apply.

Also, think about what sex is meant to achieve in terms of it being the most intimate experience of being joined with someone else that we can know – what the Bible describes as becoming 'one flesh'. This becoming one in *some way* reflects the union we have with God – that we are joined into him, and become part of his body. In the resurrection this union will be final and complete. We will look on Jesus face to face and become like him.[62] There will not be any division between us and Jesus, but we will live in the constant experience of his light and love.

---

[61] Matthew 22:30
[62] 1 John 3:2

In this joining with Jesus we will also be united perfectly with all his people. The Bible tells us that in some way this is already the case,[63] but in the resurrection it will be made perfect – you're actually going to *like* everyone else there for starters! And the good news is that this perfect relationship with Jesus and his people will be even better than sex! What sex achieves at its best – at its most beautiful and most powerful – is but a shadow of the joy we will experience in our relationship with Jesus forever.

So don't worry about the return of Jesus and the resurrection – look forward to it!

---

[63] 1 Corinthians 12:12-26

Q. If you cope with your sex drive by focusing on saving sex for marriage, what happens if you don't get married? How do you settle in for the long haul?

I think the key thing here is not so much to focus on saving sex for marriage as to focus on bringing honor to Jesus and blessing to his people whatever stage of life you are in. If your focus in life is having sex – even if you wait until married to do it – your focus is in the wrong place. You've got to live for something bigger than the urging of your gonads – you've got to live for Jesus!

If you are living full out for Jesus, seeking to bring glory to him in everything you do,[64] then the focus of everything you do will be in the right place. Whether you are married or single, the job you do, the place you live, the food you eat – all these things will be less important than pleasing Jesus, and all of them will be done to the glory of Jesus. And that is how it should be.

This doesn't mean that life is always going to be easy. I know lots of people who are single who would love to be married, and life can be tough for them – and not just because they're not getting sex. The way that we handle the tough stuff in life is by trusting in Jesus, and by receiving help from his people. God's grace is sufficient for every situation, and he places us in the family of the church so we might be encouraged and strengthened.

So don't worry about whether you will get married or not, or have sex or not. Just live flat out for Jesus!

---

[64] Colossians 3:17

Q. Are relationships only for marriage? Does it mean that you only go out with someone if you can see yourself marrying them?

Our expectations of dating are quite unusual in terms of how relationships have been conducted in most cultures. Throughout most of human history, and still today in many nations of the world, the normal thing is for a girl not to have any kind of relationship with a boy until her family decides she is ready to marry and finds a husband for her.

As I have four daughters, I think there is a lot to be said for this system!

In our culture we do things differently though, and people tend to have a number of boyfriend/girlfriend experiences before getting married. This is potentially risky, but there are a number of biblical and commonsense guidelines we can follow to keep us out of danger. My advice would be this:

Don't start dating too young. I mean, honestly, what's the point?! When you are 14 or 15 it makes far more sense to just hang out with a group of friends, of both sexes, and learn how to be friends and the kind of things that you like or dislike about members of the opposite sex. Dating just adds complications and emotional intensity to your relationships that you don't need. And just because everyone else at school is doing it doesn't mean that you have to – as a child of God you can do better than just following the crowd.

Remember that sex is only for marriage – so whatever age you are, and however serious your relationship is, don't do anything you shouldn't.

Don't get too intense in your relationship too soon. In our teen years our emotions tend to be very strong, and it is easy to get into a super intense relationship with someone, in which they fill all our thoughts and dreams. Not only will this mean that you sit drooling from the side of your mouth when you should be focusing on your math class, which is ugly and makes you look stupid, but it will not help you in your worship of Jesus.

Be real – no matter how strongly you feel for this person, if you are only 16 it is very unlikely you will end up marrying them – so don't give away more of your heart than you should.

Be relaxed. As we get older and marriage becomes a more realistic prospect relationships can get increasingly complex. I've known lots of guys get scared off by girls because they think that after going out for one coffee together they are being herded into marrying her. Sometimes this is because the guy has commitment issues, and needs to grow up. But other times it is just that there seems little space to get to know someone without everyone making the assumption you are destined to walk down the aisle together. This is silly. Chill.

To sum it all up, basically, if there is no chance of you marrying this person why bother starting a romantic relationship with them in the first place? But if there is some possibility that marriage might result don't spend all your time worrying about whether it will! Just enjoy being together, have fun, honor Jesus, and trust him to lead you where he wants you to go. If you're not right for each other finish the relationship respectfully, and move on.

Q. Should the words *I love you* be saved for marriage as well?

There are lots of contexts in which it is appropriate to say 'I love you', and not just in marriage. For instance, you should tell Jesus that you love him regularly! You should also tell your parents you love them. You might even want to tell your friends you love them. Read the Bible – it is full of instructions that we are to love one another.

However, I guess this question is asking about when you look your boyfriend/girlfriend in the eye, hold their hand, get your lips close to theirs, and whisper breathlessly, 'I luuuurve you...'

My question about this would be, 'How do you know?' If you *really* love someone then the two of you should be talking about marriage, and if you are going to marry someone of course you should tell them you love them. But if it is just that you are trying to say the right thing to make your girlfriend let you get your hand down her jeans then you shouldn't be saying it.

The reality is that it can be very difficult to know what love is until it has had time to be tried and tested. Love looks different after you've been married a few years and have experienced the ups and downs of life. I loved Grace before we got married, but I really love her now!

So I think the thing is not to rush into saying something which you're not really ready to say or the other person isn't ready to hear. Remember the instruction from the Song of Songs, not to awaken love or arouse love until you are ready. If you tell someone you love them and then a few days later decide to dump them, or they dump you, you're going to feel pretty stupid.

Q. In marriage is it alright to use condoms?

We are so used to having access to effective contraception that it is easy to not really think about it at all. But this is an important subject, and when Grace and I are doing marriage preparation with couples it is something we always talk about.

Some Christians believe that *all* contraception is wrong. These Christians tend to have very large families... They also tend to live in rural America where land is cheap and houses are big.

Most of the rest of us believe that *some* forms of contraception are acceptable – God gives us the ability to control all kinds of aspects of our bodies, and advances in medicine mean we can control a lot more than we used to be able to. And while I strongly believe that sex is meant to result in children at some point, I don't think that means we have to keep on having more and more children. I think God gives us the freedom to regulate the number of kids that we have to some degree.

But believing that God gives us this freedom also requires us to think about the kind of contraception that is appropriate. For me, the clear line on this is that contraceptives that prevent egg and sperm from meeting are acceptable, but contraceptives that destroy a fertilized egg are not. On this basis condoms are an excellent choice!

Q. Would you say that being friends or very good friends with a person before you begin a relationship benefits you both in the long run?

The person you marry should be your best friend.

Sadly, sometimes you can listen to the way married people talk and they make it sound like their marriage partner is just someone who gets in the way of them doing the things they really want to do. This shouldn't be the case. God's plan for us is that in marriage we find lifelong companionship that is very, very good.

Grace and I are friends. We like being together. We like hanging out together. We like doing stuff together. We understand one another, and are there for one another. I have lots of other friends, but Grace really is my best friend. And that's how it should be.

This doesn't mean we have to do everything together all the time. It doesn't mean that we can't get time on our own, or can't see other friends, but it does mean we always look forward to being with each other.

So if you are meant to be friends with the person you marry it seems a good idea to become friends with them before you begin a relationship. Often what attracts us to someone else is that we find them physically attractive, or we get caught up in a cloud of romance. Physical attraction and romance are important, but they don't have the same kind of staying power as real love. Real love stays strong even on those days when the person we love is not looking their best, or when life is tough and there isn't much time or energy for roses and candlelit dinners. Real love is what true friendship is about – it is knowing that this person will always be there for you, and would take a bullet for you if they had to. That is what marriage should be like.

This means that finding out if you can become friends with someone, before becoming romantically entangled with them, is probably a good idea. Do you enjoy the same kind of things? Do you make each other laugh? Do you have the same kind of values and approach to life? Can you trust them? These are all good questions to ask when making friends, and they are good questions to ask of someone you might end up marrying.

Q. What is the best age to get married? How long would you need to be in a relationship before you get married?

I'm not sure there is a 'best' age. In different cultures marriage has happened at different times. For instance, in the middle-ages a girl might get married when she was 12 or 13. In the culture of the time that was considered ok, whereas today we'd call it pedophilia.

I think in practice it is wise to wait to marry until you have done some growing up. But at the same time you don't have to have lived a lot of life to be grown up enough for marriage.

Increasingly, people wait until their 30s to get married. Why? Because they want to play the field; they want to build their career; they don't want to get tied down. None of those reasons is really a very good one for not getting married earlier. There is nothing wrong with not getting married until your 30s (or 40s, 50s, 60s...) if that is how things work out, but it is wrong to be pressed into the mold of a culture that thinks it is weird to get committed early.

A key thing is to listen to the advice of those who are older and wiser than you. Hopefully you are part of a good church with godly leaders. If so, ask them for advice. Before asking Grace to marry me I talked it through with an elder of my church – he encouraged me to go for it, so I did (at the age of 23). If your leaders bless you in the relationship you should feel free to proceed; if they don't you would be wise to back off.

In terms of how long you should be in a relationship before getting married, again there is no set time, but wisdom will suggest some guidelines. I always advise people to get to know one another for a year or so. It is worth checking out what your prospective life-long partner looks like in the winter as well as in summer! Seriously, sometimes that guy who seems all dreamy on the beach in sunny June can become grumpy and a real loser come rainy February. If you're going to spend the rest of your lives together its worth taking a few extra months to check one another out.

On the other hand, I don't think it's a good idea to spend too long in a relationship before splitting or committing. If you are boyfriend and girlfriend for five years it is unlikely that your self-control will last that long and you're going to end up sleeping together before you get married. (To be honest, if you were together that long and the temptation hadn't become overwhelming that in itself would suggest to me that you're not really meant for one another.) Grace and I were together for three years before getting married, and I think that was a year too long.

So, the key thing is to talk to your leaders and get their advice!

Q. Do you think Christians get married young so they can have sex?

Yes.

Next question?

But seriously – let's think about this a bit… If sex is good – which it definitely is – then it is totally appropriate that we should be keen to experience it with the person we are going to marry. I would be deeply concerned if a couple came to me saying they wanted to get married but had no interest in sleeping together.

The way the world thinks is that it is normal and healthy to spend your teens and 20s having sex with lots of different people and then maybe get married sometime in your 30s. But really, it is this way of thinking that is weird, rather than getting married when you are young and only ever having sex with that person.

If you have found someone you feel called to love with a lifetimes sacrificial love and if the leaders of your church bless the relationship, then why hold back?

Q. Do you think as a married couple sex is the ultimate way to express your love?

Sex is *one* way in which a married couple can express their love, but the heart of a relationship should not be sex.

Think about it this way – there may be times that a married couple cannot have sex. For instance, due to illness, or pregnancy, or whatever. Does this mean that the couple are not able to fully express love to one another? Of course not.

The ultimate way to express love for your marriage partner is to lay your life down for them. This probably won't mean literally dying for them (although it could) but it does mean that every day you choose to die to yourself in order to live sacrificially for the one you love. It is with this kind of love that Jesus loves his church, and it is with this kind of love that we should love our spouses.[65]

What this means in practice is things like thinking about the needs of your partner before your own needs. It means being there for them to help them however they need to be helped. It means that you put their interests above your own – if it's a choice between getting a great new job and damaging your marriage or saying no to that promotion to safeguard your marriage, you don't take the job. Part of this sacrificial living is then worked out sexually – that in sex you are seeking your partners pleasure more than your own.

The amazing thing about living this way is that when both partners are seeking to live sacrificially for the other both of them end up in wedded bliss! This definitely works out in sex – if both partners are seeking to make things as pleasurable for each other as they possible can, then both end up very happy! This is how God has designed us to work – we really are at our happiest when we are living most generously.

In this sacrificial way of living all that you do with your marriage partner becomes an expression of ultimate love. When you choose to do that household chore that neither of you like doing, that is a sacrificial act, and a sign of ultimate love. When you don't buy

---

[65] Ephesians 5:22-33

something you would like in order to be able to buy something your partner would like, that is a sacrificial act, and a sign of ultimate love. When you refuse to be led into sexual temptation with someone to whom you are not married, that is a sacrificial act, and a sign of ultimate love. And when you make love to your marriage partner, as a sacrificial act it becomes a sign of ultimate love.

Q. Is it sinful to lust after your boyfriend or girlfriend?

Biblically speaking, lust is always presented as something negative. Lust is about desiring something that is not yours to have. Lust is unhealthy desire. Lust is destructive because acting on it always means violating God's laws and other peoples rights. In the end, lust leads to our destruction. Proverbs tells us that, "The righteousness of the upright delivers them, but the treacherous are taken captive by their lust."[66] And Jesus said that to look at a woman lustfully is to commit adultery with her.[67]

Because lust is always negative, we need to learn to distinguish it from those desires that are appropriate and healthy. For example, it is right to desire food when you are hungry, drink when you are thirsty, and sleep when you are tired. These are desires God gives us in order to stay healthy. But it is wrong when these desires get distorted – when our desire for food becomes gluttony, or our desire for drink drunkenness, or our desire for sleep laziness.

In a similar way, it is right for a husband and wife to desire one another sexually, but it is wrong to have this desire towards someone you are not married to. Practically, this might mean that a husband carries a picture of his wife in the nude with him when he is away from home because he has a right to see and desire his wife. But carrying a picture of a woman who is not his wife would be lust, and wrong!

So where does this leave you in how you should feel about your boyfriend or girlfriend? Obviously, there is meant to be physical attraction between you. It would be really weird to have a relationship with someone if you didn't fancy them! But where is the line that means you have crossed into sinful lust?

This becomes even more of a problem if you are going to get married, and the closer you get to the wedding day. I remember when Grace and I were engaged being given a book about sexual technique in order to help prepare us for when we were married. I didn't know *what* I was supposed to do with that as all it did was make me think even more about Grace's soft skin than I had been

---

[66] Proverbs 11:6
[67] Matthew 5:28

already – was I allowed to be thinking about her this way? As we were engaged was it ok to now start fantasizing about sex? Was I lusting sinfully or staying on the straight and narrow?

You may well be experiencing something similar as you read this book. It has been written to help you understand more of God's purpose for sex so you might stay pure for him. But chances are that all this information about sex is making you think about sex all the more, and might not be helping you at all. That's the trouble with sex – it is so immensely powerful that whether we talk about it or try and ignore it we can get led into lust.

So how are we going to answer this question about lusting after your boy/girlfriend?

I think the first thing is realizing that it is lustful – and therefore sin – to desire anything that you are not entitled to. And the reality is, you are not entitled to the body of your boy/girlfriend. Until you have come into the covenant relationship of marriage with someone you have no rights over their body. You therefore need to be doing everything you can to kill lust – or it will kill you. In a boyfriend/girlfriend relationship this means not doing anything that stirs up passions in you that you should not be experiencing.

But perhaps an even more important thing than recognizing what lust is, is seeking to have a heart that runs faithfully in pursuit of Jesus over and above anything else. If your number one desire is to live in a way that pleases him, then lust is going to get squeezed out of your way of thinking. And this means that rather than lusting after the person you are dating you will be seeking Jesus as to how you can best honor him and bless them.

Having your heart directed this way doesn't mean that you will no longer feel sexual attraction or desire, but it will mean that those desires are kept under control. It means that you will be able to shepherd those desires and keep them where they are meant to be, just like a farmer herds a flock of willful sheep so they all stay in the place where they are safe.

And if you do get married, having your heart directed in the right direction will mean that you are not bringing lust to bed, but pure and passionate desire for your marriage partner which you offer to them as a sacrifice of love – and not merely as a way to satisfy your own selfishness.

Q. My parents relationship came out of an adulterous relationship and I feel like I'm living in sin. What shall I do?

The Old Testament gives us a clear principle on this one, where it says, "Fathers shall not be put to death because of their children, nor shall children be put to death because of their fathers. Each one shall be put to death for his own sin."[68]

Basically, what this means is that each of us are accountable for our own actions – and this means you are not answerable for what your parents have done.

If you were born because your parents had an adulterous affair it is very easy to carry a sense of guilt about this. Anyone who has been told that they were a mistake, or were never wanted, or has been born as a result of rape, or any other relationship which was not what it should have been, can easily end up feeling burdened and ashamed. If this is you, it is important to look these accusations in the eye, acknowledge their power, but then proclaim the greater power of Jesus' death and resurrection over them.

Satan is a liar, and he will use any route he can to speak lies to us. We need to recognize and reject his lies. What your parents did is not your fault. It is not your responsibility. You will not have to answer for it.

What is true is that each of us has sinned and stands in need of God's grace and forgiveness.[69] If we have turned in faith to Christ he is more than able to give us this grace and forgiveness. On the cross Jesus paid the price for our sin and carried the wrath of his Father for it. He also took our shame, so that we need no longer be under the bondage of the sins that have been committed against us. So when Satan whispers lies to us we need to look to the cross again and declare its power over our lives – Jesus has broken the power of sin over us. Listen to what God speaks over you, not the lies of the devil. To God you are precious and adopted as his child.[70] There is no condemnation for those who are in Christ Jesus.[71]

---

[68] Deuteronomy 24:16
[69] Romans 3:23
[70] Ephesians 1:5
[71] Romans 8:1

Very practically, we also need to seek to honor our parents. This is a biblical command,[72] but like all the commands we need to know the help of the Holy Spirit if we are going to keep it. Often it is much easier to be aware of all the screw ups and failings of our parents and to bitch and moan about them. Instead, what we need to do is seek God's blessing for them, and be quick to praise them wherever we see anything that reflects our Father in heaven – even if it is only the tiniest glimpse.

---

[72] Exodus 20:12

Q. If it is adultery to involve a third person in sex, is IVF adultery?

If a woman in my church came to me because her husband had a low sperm count and asked me to quickly impregnate her because she wanted a baby, would that be adultery? What if it was all over in seconds and completely lacking in passion or emotional connection, and done for the best of motives? Even then, I don't think there would be much doubt: it would still be adultery. I wouldn't be merely a donor. I would have done something that should not be done and I would – rightly – lose my job.

IVF is a very sensitive subject. For those couples who cannot conceive, the emotional pain can be unbelievably intense. Believe me – this is one of the most painful things I have to deal with as a pastor, and its intensity should never be underestimated. If a couple carrying this pain have gone the route of IVF and used donated eggs or sperm and had a beautiful baby as a result they are likely to be very sensitive about being told they have done something wrong. And if you were that baby this is going to be a very sensitive subject for you too.

Being sensitive to this sensitivity doesn't mean we should ignore ethical reality though.

While IVF does not involve physical contact, it is far more than simply shuffling a few cells around in a laboratory. How about if I didn't actually have sex with that woman whose husband had a low sperm count – and just donated some sperm that a doctor then used to fertilize one of her eggs? Any resulting child would still be my child – just as certainly as if I had had sex with the woman. What I had done would still in some way be adulterous because my sperm and the woman's eggs were never meant to come in contact with each other, because we were not in the covenant of marriage together.

This means I could never encourage or counsel an infertile couple to use IVF if it involved the genetic material of a third person. As well as the adultery problem, there are other problems that mean we should approach IVF cautiously, even if it uses only the husband

and wife's sperm and eggs. This is a very complex area, but the kind of things I would be concerned about are:

- IVF often results in 'spare' embryos that are then discarded or destroyed.
- IVF often results in several embryos being implanted in the mother, and this frequently causes complications of premature delivery, death of one or more of the babies, and other health issues.
- There is increasing evidence that babies conceived by IVF have significantly more health problems than normally conceived infants.

While not being able to have a baby can be unbelievably distressing for a couple, none of us actually has a right to have children. It is only by the grace of God that any of us is able to do so, and for those couples who not able to conceive it may be that God's intention is to use them to bless other people in a different way from those who have children. For instance, one of the most beautiful things a childless couple can do is to adopt other children. This is often a difficult and costly path to walk, but it reflects the father heart of God, who has adopted us into his family, at the terrible cost of the cross.

Q. Is adoption alright for infertile couples?

Adoption is a wonderful thing for infertile couples to do – and also for those couples who have their own children but find sufficient grace in God to care for more.

Adoption is a very biblical principle. The Bible is full of language that describes God's relationship with his people to be one of adoption. The people of Israel were adopted as God's sons[73] and to be a Christian means being adopted by God.[74] Adoption is to deliberately choose a child who has been orphaned or abandoned and to give them a home and all the rights and privileges of family membership. To be adopted by God means we are no longer spiritual orphans but those who will inherit all the riches of heaven. To be adopted by a human family means being chosen to be as genuinely part of that family as if you had been born into it. Adoption is good!

---

[73] Romans 9:4
[74] Ephesians 1:5

Q. So what should gay people do if they want a family? Naturally marrying the opposite sex would be silly as you would not be physically attracted to them. How do you respond to gay couples with children or wanting to adopt? How do you then respond to the children?

Whether gay people should adopt is a complicated matter. In some jurisdictions of the USA, in the UK, and in a number of other countries, gay couples have as much legal right to adopt as anyone else. I would view this as less than ideal as it does not represent a biblically valid model of family life. At the same time it is arguably better for children to be adopted by a loving gay couple, than to be passed from one foster home to another. Clearly, in terms of how we handle things in the church, we would not be encouraging gay people to live together in the first place, so adoption would not be the main issue to address anyway.

An interesting question is whether people who are *single* and *celibate* should adopt (regardless of whether they are gay or straight).

If someone is a single parent because their partner has died, or their relationship has fallen apart, we would not say that they shouldn't be parents. (Although where people have had inappropriate relationships and had a baby as a result we might say it would have been better if they had never got themselves into that situation.) We certainly wouldn't want the child to feel in anyway second rate or stigmatized. What we would want is for the community of the church to help provide the help that the parent and child need. For example, a single mom in the church should be getting help from men in the church who are able to look out for her kids and do some of the things a dad would do.

At the same time we would want to stick firmly to the principle that the ideal thing for kids is to have both mum and dad around. This means that we would not encourage single people to adopt, in the same way that we wouldn't encourage single women to get pregnant.

However, in some African countries where there are huge numbers of orphans because of HIV/AIDS we might see it as appropriate for single people to adopt – but in this kind of situation there would be a special responsibility on the rest of the church to get really stuck in and help. Ideally the church should operate like a big family, where moms and dads have primary responsibility for raising children, but where other adults – married or single, gay or straight – are also involved in caring for those children like aunts and uncles.

None of us actually has the right to have children. We tend to think we do, because we tend to think in terms of *my rights*, but this isn't how the Bible describes children. In the Bible, children are not a right, but a blessing, that God allows parents to enjoy. Sometimes our situation in life means that we don't get to enjoy certain blessings. And sometimes the choices we make in one area of our lives means we don't get to choose something else we would like in another area.

Now someone who is gay might respond by saying, "My sexual orientation wasn't my choice! But I still want kids!" I can understand that. But that understanding doesn't mean that it is then right to go about getting kids you shouldn't have. What it does mean is that the body of the church has a responsibility to help all its members handle the pain they carry. As Christians we are guaranteed suffering – this may not sound very cheerful, but the point is that in our suffering we are meant to understand the glory that is going to be ours.[75] Whether someone is gay or straight, if they want children and can't have them this is extraordinarily painful. Being part of a church means allowing others to help you carry that pain.

Of course, if a gay couple already have children and start coming to church, you don't reject the children, or the couple! In a situation like this there will be a whole range of issues for the couple and the church to work out together, and the main responsibility of church members will be to demonstrate the love of God.

---

[75] Romans 8:18

Q. Nobody ever talks about sex within marriage, what if it gets boring?!

This depends on what church you go to! In a healthy church there should be an appropriate openness about sex, and an expectation that married couples will enjoy this aspect of their relationship.

It is easy to worry that sex will get boring if you just do it with one person. Our culture conditions us to expect things to get boring if we keep doing them. The way a consumer culture works is to make us dissatisfied with the thing we already have so we go out and spend money buying something else. Our TV shows and movies also spread the message that sexual excitement is found in moving from relationship to relationship, rather than staying faithfully with one person.

As followers of Jesus we need to retrain our minds so that we think differently from our culture. We need to learn that faithfulness is good, and faithfulness is satisfying. Our relationships should not be like microwave meals, but something substantial and solid.

So how does sex work in marriage over the long haul?

First up, sex *can* get boring in marriage. But then it can get boring if you are not married too. Just take a look at the magazines written for women in their 50's – it's all stuff about how to recapture the spark in your love life, the shine in your shimmer, the zest in your zinger!

But sex doesn't have to become boring. The great advantage of faithfully having sex with the same person year after year is that you should both get better and better at it as you get to know one another more and more. With practice, a married couple should be able to bring one another increasing sexual pleasure the more they know and understand one another. Married couples need to work hard at keeping romance alive in their relationship. If a couple are daily living in sacrificial love for one another, communicating together, and making time for each other, then it is likely that their sex life will be a good one.

Don't let the lies our culture tells us about sex put you off marriage. Marriage is actually the best place to have sex. Married couples have the best sex!

Q. What would you say about a relationship when one party is significantly older than the other?

Not much.

Obviously, if a 30 year-old guy was hanging around the 16 year-old girls in my church I would be concerned. I would want to check him out and see if he needed a knee to the groin. But other than that, it really depends on whether or not the couple are well matched.

It is not unusual for a guy in his 20s to get attracted to a girl in her teens. Sometimes this is not healthy, and the guy needs the knee to groin treatment, but other times it all works out fine. In this kind of situation it is appropriate that the parents of the girl and the leaders of the church exercise cautious oversight of the situation, but I have known couples like this who were made for each other. If she is 16 and he 26 you're going to have to get used to some comments – but a few years down the line when she is 26 and he 36 no-one even notices anymore.

I'm guessing that the person asking this question is in a situation where one person is in their teens and the other in their 20's. If that's the case, just take extra care because it is easier for the older person to manipulate the younger one. Listen to those who are older and wiser than you, and invite them to speak into your relationship – check it out with some mature people in your church and follow their advice.

You also need to be aware of the changes you go through as you leave your teens and enter your 20's. You will be a very different person when you are 26 than you are at 16, and it might be that the guy who looked so sophisticated and interesting ten years earlier is actually a bit of a jerk. That's not a mistake you want to make.

Q. If using pornography prevents you from having sex before marriage, is it really that bad?

I'm going to assume that what this question means is:
1. That you use porn in response to, and in order to heighten, sexual arousal
2. Which leads to masturbation
3. Which provides an orgasm
4. Which means sexual desire is being met
5. So you don't actually have sex with someone else.

This is not good!

For starters, looking at porn is a way of entertaining lust, and lust is bad. Lust is looking on something which is not yours to have with a desire that is wrong. Jesus said that looking at a woman this way is as bad as if you were actually sleeping with her.[76] The way to fight sin is not by doing another sin – kidding yourself that you are being somehow virtuous by perving over pornographic images while refraining from sleeping with someone is just a joke.

Another problem with the "porn helps keep me sexually pure" myth is that it encourages selfishness. If you become habituated to getting sexual pleasure through looking at porn and masturbating yourself it is going to be much more difficult for you to enjoy a healthy sex life with your partner once you are married. Porn demands nothing of you – it is just there for your pleasure. But real sex demands a sacrificial attitude towards your partner. Unlike the images in porn, a real person has real desires and needs and preferences of their own – and this is going to come as a nasty shock if you have trained yourself to believe that sex is simply about your personal gratification. It will make you lousy in bed.

As followers of Jesus we do not fight sin with sin, and we do not even just try and bottle up our temptations by not acting upon them. Instead we renew our minds daily so that we do God's will[77] and we live in a way that honors Jesus and blesses other people. This is the whole point of Jesus saying that looking at a woman lustfully is as much adultery as actually getting into bed with her –

---

[76] Matthew 5:28
[77] Romans 12:2

as Christians we are not merely about regulating behavior, but changing hearts.

We have to get to the place where sexual temptation does not control us, but where we can look it square in the face, see what it really is, and walk away in freedom. Habitual porn use is not freedom, but slavery to lust. We are not meant to be slaves, because in Christ we have been declared to be free.[78]

---

[78] Romans 6:17-18

Q. What would be your response to a married couple who use pornography as part of their sex life? Is it a sign of problems within their marriage?

The book of Proverbs says that a man should let his wife's breasts fill him with delight at all times.[79] So, if a man needs someone else's breasts to turn him on, then – yes – there is something wrong in the marriage.

Lust and virtual adultery don't cease to be lust and adultery because you are doing it while your marriage partner is with you. Using porn in marriage is adultery, and it defiles the marriage bed.[80] Just because it is on the screen doesn't make it morally any different from if a married couple decided to invite some other people into their bed for an orgy.

Husband and wife should be attracted enough by one another not to need outside stimulus for their sex life. If they are not attracted to each other in this way then there are underlying problems in their relationship that need to be talked through and changed.

Sex is one of the unifying bonds of marriage and in the bedroom husband and wife should see things and do things that only they see and do. Their sexual relationship should be unique and exclusively between them, and help them to grow deeper in love for one another. Watching porn together is not going to help this.

---

[79] Proverbs 5:19
[80] Hebrews 13:4

Q. Does God condone reporting your sexual abuser if they are a parent? As this breaks a commandment?

I guess the commandment you are referring to is the one to honor your father and mother?[81] This commandment does set out an important principle for how we should treat our parents. It means we should be respectful and obedient towards them. It means we should want the best for them. But in the context of the biblical story it also assumes that parents act with covenant love towards their children – just as God does towards his people.

Old Testament law makes it very clear that parents and children should not have sex with one another.[82] The Old Testament also repeatedly stresses that one of the worst things a parent could do is offer their child in sacrifice to false gods.[83] In the book of Ephesians Paul quotes the command that children should honor their parents, but then adds the instruction that parents should not, "provoke your children to anger, but bring them up in the discipline and instruction of the Lord."[84]

All this makes it very clear that parents have a responsibility before God in how they treat their children, just as children have a responsibility before God in how they treat their parents. For a parent to sexually abuse their child is for them to break the covenant they are meant to keep with their child. They are in effect sacrificing their child to the false god of sexual desire and abusive control. They are failing to bring them up in the instruction of the Lord. In such a case, there is a responsibility upon the wider community to bring the abuser to justice. In the Old Testament this meant that a parent who sacrificed their child to Molech had to be killed.[85] In our context, the appropriate thing to do is that the relevant authorities should become involved.

If a parent is sexually abusing you, to report them is not to break a commandment. Biblically, it is absolutely the right thing to do.

---

[81] Exodus 20:12
[82] See Leviticus 18
[83] For example, see Leviticus 20:1-5
[84] Ephesians 6:1-4
[85] Leviticus 20

Sexual abusers typically exert power over their victims by threatening all sorts of terrible consequences if anyone is told about the abuse. This means that often abuse continues unchecked for a long time. Often victims of sexual abuse are made to feel that is they who are the guilty ones, rather than the abuser, and that to tell anyone about the abuse will compound their guilt.

All of this is lies.

If you are being abused, you *must* tell someone. You have got to report the abuse, in order that you might get free.

Q. What about Abraham sleeping with his servant? How did that honor marriage?

It didn't!

In Genesis 16 we read about how in her desperation to have a child, Abram's wife Sarai (this was before God updated their names to Abraham and Sarah) gave her servant Hagar to Abram. The idea behind this was that any child Hagar had by Abram would in effect be Sarai's child – Hagar belonged to Sarai, so Hagar's baby was Sarai's baby.

Trouble was, as soon as Hagar fell pregnant she began to feel superior to Sarai, and Sarai started to hate her. Pretty soon everyone is playing the blame game, with Sarai declaring to her husband, "May the wrong done to me be on you!"[86]

Abraham bedding his servant caused no end of hassle and stands as one of the great mistakes in Abe's walk of faith. It caused marital tension between him and his wife. It caused Hagar to rebel against her mistress. It caused Sarah to abuse her servant. It led to the child – Ishmael – never having the closeness of relationship with his father that he should have had. And generations later it led to conflict between Abe's descendants as the people of Israel and the people of Ishmael fought one another – a state of affairs that persists to this day in the battle between Jew and Arab.

We also see Abe's grandson Jacob making the same kind of mistakes, as his wives enter a reproductive arms race,[87] trying to outcompete one another through their own and their servants wombs. Sadly, both Abraham and Jacob were typical men and happy enough to sleep with extra women when the opportunity presented itself, but the results were not happy.

What these stories of the patriarchs show us is that when God's plan of marriage being between one man and one woman is ignored, trouble always ensues. The good news is that in his grace God is able to bring good things out of the mess, but that doesn't

---

[86] Genesis 16:5
[87] See Genesis 29:31 – 30:22

mean we should deliberately put ourselves in a messy situation in the first place.

Getting our sexual relationships right is so important that by the time we come to the New Testament the Apostle Paul makes it a required qualification that anyone who wants to be an elder has to be a one woman man.[88] Abraham is our example in faith, but his relationship with Hagar is more of a warning, and not something for us to copy.

---

[88] 1 Timothy 3:2; Titus 1:6

Q. Is it wrong to date someone in another country, E.g., UK & USA?

No, but it can be tricky.

A lot depends on how and where you meet. Sometimes people hook up across continents through internet dating. The trouble then is that it is not that straightforward to meet up if you want to develop a proper relationship. If you start dating while at college or something and then one person returns to their home country, or if they move to another country to work or study, you are both going to have to make some big decisions.

Marrying someone who is from another culture always adds complexity to a relationship – even when it is two relatively similar cultures like those of the US and UK. There isn't necessarily anything wrong with this, it is just something that needs to be born in mind – if you are not prepared to learn about someone else's culture and accommodate yourself to it then don't get into a relationship with someone from a different culture.

Moving to a different nation to be with the one you love can also be complex. Even if it is absolutely the right thing to do there will still be a cost involved. My brother and his family live in Chicago, while one of Grace's brothers and his wife live in Sao Paulo. This means we never see them! If you don't like your family this may sound an attractive option, but if you like your family you will find it tough.

Q. Did Adam and Eves children commit incest? And if they did, how is that ok?

The first way to answer this question is to acknowledge that it is impossible to give a definite answer! The Bible just doesn't tell us what the deal was here, and where the Bible doesn't tell us something plainly it is best not to get too dogmatic about our interpretation of it.

But that being said, we can make some guesses about where Cain found his wife.

There are really only two significant possibilities. The first is that in the very early days of creation, incest was permitted to allow the human race to spread and increase as fast as possible. Genesis tells us that Eve was made from Adam,[89] so they were presumably genetically very similar, and those genes were uncorrupted – from this pure gene pool the whole human race was to descend.

Also, what we now call incest wouldn't even have been thought of in those terms. If the only people around were Adam and Eve and their kids they wouldn't have all been looking at each other in the same way that we look at our parents and brothers and sisters!

How we feel about incest is to a large extent shaped by the culture we live in. Some cultures have very strict rules about marrying even very distant relatives, while other cultures are more relaxed. For example, in the UK you are allowed to marry your cousin, because Henry VIII changed the law to allow this so that he could marry his! In the Middle East cousin marriage is common, while in several of the American states it is forbidden, with Texas making it against the law in 2005.

In the Bible we read that Abraham was married to his half-sister[90] but by the time we get to the law of Moses this kind of relationship was forbidden.[91] Of course, Abraham and Sarah lived several hundred years before God gave their descendants the law, so the culture they lived in was very different.

---

[89] Genesis 2:21-22
[90] See Genesis 20
[91] See Leviticus 18

All this means that it is totally possible that Cain married his sister but that it wasn't really incest as we would describe it.

The second possibility is that God created other people, not biologically descended from Adam and Eve, and one of these married Cain. This is often the view of those who believe in theistic-evolution, rather than a literal six day creation – so in the end, what you believe about how God made the world will determine how you answer the question of where Cain found his wife.

Q. Where can Christians go to learn about sex, sort sexual issues in marriage, and get support if no one's talking about it?!

Really this is an issue for local churches – church should be a place where we can talk about all kinds of things, including sex.

Church is a lot like family. The way that families handle sex can often be unhelpful – this can range from the most extreme, where one family member sexually abuses another, to less serious but still significant problems, like sex being a subject parents are too embarrassed to discuss with their kids, or it only ever being referred to in a joking way rather than taken seriously. Churches can be like this too – church leaders might not mention sex because they are embarrassed, or afraid of offending certain church members, or because their own sex lives are rubbish.

But this is not how it should be.

In my family we try to be as open about sex as we can – in a way that is appropriate for our children to hear. Grace and I want our kids to learn about sex from us, not just from the lyrics of pop songs or the things their friends tell them or from biology lessons at school. And we want them to be able to talk to us about sex and relationships without it feeling uncomfortable or weird.

Church life should be like this. Sex is something that affects everyone, whatever age they are and whether or not they are married. Sex really is a community issue, so it is something that should be taught about in community.

A lot of this talk does have to go on in private. It might be that the pastor of your church is spending a lot of time talking with people about sexual issues in their marriages, or with single people about their struggles, but you are not aware of this because it would be totally wrong for him to stand up on a Sunday and say, "This week I saw Mr & Mrs Smith on Monday to discuss with them why he is not meeting her sexual needs. And then on Thursday I saw Mr & Mrs Jones who want a baby but his sperm count is too low. On Friday I saw young Jack over there who has a serious masturbation problem." You just don't need that kind of information!

But there should be things going on and being said that make it clear that sex is not a taboo area in your church. For instance, are couples who get engaged then getting proper marriage preparation counseling? Does sex ever get mentioned – when it is appropriate – during sermons? Is there an emphasis upon living in purity, with practical and honest discussion of what that looks like and why it is difficult? Are marriage and family life talked about and honored?

If these kind of things are not going on in your church, then there might be a problem. If so, it is a problem that needs to get resolved. If it is not resolved then (and I write this extremely cautiously) maybe you should be looking for another church.

Q. If you knew you were going to die soon and you didn't have time to find a partner but you wanted to experience sex would it be so wrong to use a dildo?

If you knew you were about to die I think you would suddenly find there were more important things for you to worry about than sex!

Maybe the fact that you were about to meet your Maker might get you focused on ensuring that your heart attitude to him was right, rather than desperately trying to get your end away.

Q. In the eyes of God, are rape victims still virgins?

This is a difficult question to answer.

In the literal, physical sense, anyone who has had sex – whether voluntarily or otherwise – is no longer a virgin. But the Bible makes it very clear that sex is not just a physical matter, but about the attitude of our hearts. As Jesus put it, in the verse we keep quoting,[92] to look lustfully at a woman is to commit adultery with her.

So, you may technically be a virgin, but if you and your boyfriend have kissed and cuddled each other to the point where you have had an orgasm are you really still virgins? Not really. Or even if you haven't done this, but have simply fantasized about having sex with someone, while you are still a virgin in your body, you are not one in your heart.

Sex is not just biology.

But what if you really are a virgin, and get raped? How does God then view you?

The first thing to be clear on is that the blame, guilt and shame rest with the rapist, not you. Rape is a hideous sin. It offends against God and it offends against all that human relationships are meant to be.

One of the bleakest moments in Israel's history involved a rape. It was a rape that vividly displayed how the nation needed to come under godly rule rather than living in the moral anarchy of the times. In this story (told in Judges 19 – 21) a man's concubine is hideously raped, to the point where she dies, by men of the tribe of Benjamin. In revenge, the rest of Israel go to war against the Benjamites and kill 25,000 of them.

In another shocking story, King David's son Amnon rapes his half-sister Tamar. In revenge Tamar's full-brother Absolom kills Amnon, and there is then a whole sorry mess that results. (You can read about this in 2 Samuel 13.)

---

[92] Matthew 5:28

One of the things that stands out from these stories is that it is very definitely the men who carry out the rape who are guilty, and it is the men who are punished.

If you have been the victim of rape it is not you who are guilty.

In the eyes of God, it is whether we are regarded as guilty or righteous that is really the key thing, not whether or not we are virgins. Because of what Jesus has done, a victim of rape can stand spotless before God. On the cross Jesus carried the sins we have done, and also the shame of what has been done to us. Because of the cross each of us can know what it means to be covered by the righteousness of Christ.

This means that a rape victim can stand before God *as if* they were a virgin. The Bible tells us that Jesus died for our sin, but was raised to life for our justification.[93] To be justified means that God counts us as righteous – there is no charge against us to answer. One way we can express this is to say that being justified is like being able to say, *it's 'just as if I'd' never sinned*. This also means that the sins that have been committed against us lose their power. It means a rape victim can say, 'I know Jesus sees me as clean and complete, not dirty and broken.'

---

[93] Romans 4:25

Q. What if you get raped? You wouldn't still want to save sex for marriage if it was taken from you already?

Sadly, many people who have been sexually abused respond to this by becoming sexually promiscuous themselves. It is easy to understand why this might happen – if what you have learnt through your experiences is that the only value you have is what others can get from you sexually, then it is likely that you will use sex as a means to try and get others to value you. If something so intimate and private as sex has been forced upon you, then why bother trying to keep it intimate and private in the future?

This response is totally understandable. But it is wrong.

Rather than seeing your body as just a piece of plumbing that other people can make use of if they want to, you need to see yourself as God sees you. Rather than trying to win love and approval from others by letting them use you sexually, you need to understand the love and approval that God has for you. Rather than believing you are fatally corrupted and messed up, you need to understand what it means to be a new creation in Christ Jesus.

The way out of the damage that sexual abuse and rape causes is not to damage yourself further by living in a way that is contrary to what God intends for you.

Sexual promiscuity in response to sexual abuse becomes a self-fulfilling negative prophecy. If you make yourself sexually available you will end up just getting taken advantage of again. You will make yourself less attractive to a godly partner and an obvious target for those who have no real interest in you, but only in gratifying their own lust.

The healing process from rape and sexual abuse is often long and painful, but there really is healing available. If you can learn what it means that God sees you as righteous and has justified you, you will be able to train your mind to understand why what you do with your body has significance. If you can come to grips with the truth that in Christ you are a new creation,[94] then you will not succumb to the lie that you are worthless.

A young woman I know was sexually abused as a child and as a consequence made herself widely available to boys when she was a teenager. In the end she came to understand how Jesus viewed her, and the healing that could be hers and stopped selling herself to anyone who seemed to be offering some affection. Now she is married to an amazing man, who is passionate about her and views her as pure and lovely – which she is.

Sex is always worth saving for marriage. If you have been raped you may be struggling to see the preciousness of sex, but God can help you to see it again.

---

94 2 Corinthians 5:17

Conclusion: fighting lust with the full armor of God

One of the questions most often asked about sex is, "How can I get free from lust?" I want to finish this book with some advice as to how we can fight this enemy – and win!

The first thing we need to understand is the strategy of our enemy, and with lust it is really very simple – the way that lust works is to make us fixate on something we shouldn't so that we come under its power. Paul writes to the Ephesians that our fight is against spiritual rulers and authorities – the principalities and powers – not against flesh and blood.[95] The principalities and powers of lust have us under their control when our minds become obsessed with the object of our lust. We are truly free from lust only when the principalities and powers have no effect on us.

For a man looking at porn, a woman's breasts might be regarded as 'principalities and powers'! Imagine you are on your computer, not looking for porn, but searching for something else. And then a picture of some principalities and powers pops up. How do you respond?

To make the scenario a bit more juicy, imagine this happens when your mother, or girlfriend, or wife, are in the room with you. What do you do?

Jesus says that to look on a woman lustfully is to commit adultery with her,[96] and Paul says that we should flee sexual immorality.[97] So, clearly, sitting there with your tongue hanging our salivating over those wonderful principalities and powers is not in line with what the Bible teaches us!

But imagine – because your mother/girlfriend/wife is there – you shut that page down as quickly as you can, and pretend you never saw it. Does that mean you are free from lust? No it doesn't, not if your mind keeps turning back to the image. Real freedom is when

---

[95] Ephesians 5:10-18
[96] Matthew 5:28
[97] 1 Corinthians 6:18

you can look at the principalities and powers full on, but, protected by the armor of God, move on without them getting their hooks in you.

Real freedom is when you genuinely don't want the thing that would tempt you to lust. You are truly free when you can look at the temptation and know that what it offers is not so good as what being obedient to Jesus offers.

Real freedom means that you can look at a pretty girl and simply see that she is pretty, without starting to undress her with your eyes and fantasizing about what it would be like to take her to bed. (Obviously, I'm writing from a man's perspective here – but the same principles apply for women too.) The same kind of thing is in operation when it comes to non-sexual desires. For example, it's when you can see something in a shop (a Ferrari, latest iPod, cool clothes, whatever) and are able to say, "That's nice," and then walk on by, without becoming obsessed with having that thing.

Paul tells the Ephesians that the way they are going to have victory over the principalities and powers is by going into battle wearing the right kit.[98] If you are struggling with porn, or with looking at people lustfully, real freedom comes when you are able to "stand firm" wearing the full armor of God. Let's take a look at how this works out...

The belt of truth

The truth of what Jesus has done needs to be something that surrounds you – this is the truth that speaks of Jesus' redeeming blood shed for you, and his claim on your life.

One of the ways lust works is by telling us lies. This is the way that all temptation works at its most basic – it tells you that succumbing to the temptation will make life easier/better/happier. That is why temptation is tempting! Of course, the reality is different. Succumbing to temptation and entering the way of sin often does make life feel easier or better or happier – at least for a time – but

---

[98] Ephesians 6:10-18

the end result is always to do you harm and to distance you from God.

Lust's power is that it tells you that indulging it will bring you satisfaction. Obeying lust will make life easier – because it does feel easier to give in to lust than to fight it – lust just feels so strong. And lust tells you it will make life better, because you were made to indulge your sexual desires. And lust tells you that it will make you happier, because what could possibly leave you feeling better than sex?

But this is all lies!

Where lust leads us is into destructiveness. It pollutes our relationships with other people and with God. In the end it doesn't make life easier, better or happier but turns us into zombies.

The way to fight lies is with truth. Every time lust whispers a lie to you, you need to fight it with truth. You need to be belted with truth because the lies of lust will come at you from all directions and without a good belt you're going to lose your pants! Too many Christians walk around with the spiritual equivalent of skater dude jeans – hanging halfway down their backsides with their underwear showing. This is not cool.

So, keep your pants on with the belt of truth! When that lustful lie whispers in your ear send it packing with a truthful response. Declare what Jesus has done for you, and how his promises are better and more satisfying than lusts lies.

The breastplate of righteousness

The righteousness of Jesus protects your heart from temptation. A Roman soldier going into battle had to protect his chest – he was going to face the enemy, and didn't want to get a spear between the ribs. That is what a breastplate is for. (If you are a girl, you could also think of this as being the thing that protects your breasts – they are not meant to be touched by anyone but your husband!)

Righteousness is given to us when we turn to Jesus in faith. Paul goes so far in his letter to the Romans as to write that we are "slaves of righteousness."[99] Righteousness is meant to be the thing that defines us.

Now, it is important to understand that being righteous isn't the same thing as being a dork. True righteousness is not about being 'holier-than-thou'. Instead, real righteousness is about being like Christ and doing what he wants us to do. Lots of people wear *WWJD* bracelets, but these are pretty wussy compared with a breastplate! Think of a breastplate of righteousness as being a great slab of protective Kevlar strapped to your chest. Wrapped in that stuff lust is just going to bounce off.

So how do we get this piece of kit on and into action?

Paul says that it happens when rather than "presenting our members" (the parts of our bodies) to sin, we present them to righteousness.[100] This means we have to make deliberate choices about what we do with our bodies. It means we exercise the choice not to fix our eyes on porn, and masturbate ourselves, but to get on our knees and pray, or get on our feet and dance before the Lord.

The key thing here is to understand that you do have the choice about what you do. Because we have "died to sin"[101] we have the freedom to say "No!" to temptation. No Christian can ever say, "I couldn't help myself." That is a lie, because in Christ you could!

So when you are tempted by lust you have a choice – strap on the Kevlar, or get knifed in the ribs.

---

[99] Romans 6:18
[100] Romans 6:19
[101] Romans 6:1-7

Shoes of the gospel

These are really cool shoes that will carry you in safety into good places, doing the will of God.

When I go for a run I put running shoes on. If I'm chopping wood I put steel-toed boots on. Being a Christian involves a lot of running and axe-swinging, because Christian life is a fight. If you want to spend your whole life mincing around in Jimmy Choo's you're going to end up missing a few toes or breaking your ankle.

Paul says that putting on gospel shoes means putting on "readiness".[102] Readiness is going to help you avoid lust because it means you are ready to flee for your life[103] when lust comes looking for you. The book of Proverbs describes "a young man lacking sense" who wanders into the arms of another man's wife, with terrible results.[104] It is easy to wander through life and for lust to whack us round the head and knock us of our feet just because we weren't ready for it. A soldier going in to battle is ready for a fight. He's got the right shoes on. He's not going to be taken by surprise.

Wearing gospel shoes helps us fight lust as it means we are on the alert for temptation. The man wearing gospel shoes is on the alert every time he switches on a computer, flicks on the TV or opens a magazine. A woman wearing gospel shoes has her wits about her every time a guy offers to buy her a drink or drive her home.

Gospel shoes carry you out of trouble.

The shield of faith

Before we invented bullets and explosive, battles were fought hand to hand, with bits of metal and lumps of wood. But there could be a lot of sophistication in those bits of metal and lumps of wood, which meant some armies were much more successful than others.

---

[102] Ephesians 6:15
[103] 1 Corinthians 6:18
[104] Proverbs 7

One recurring lesson learnt in the history of warfare was that an infantry force could be hugely successful by carrying big shields.

That might seem obvious. After all, if you want to avoid getting hit, it's good to have something big and solid to shelter behind. But it's not actually that obvious, because the disadvantage of a big shield is that it can stop you from moving so fast – something big and heavy enough to absorb an arrow or sword strike is going to be pretty weighty. This meant that those armies which effectively used big shields were those who were highly disciplined, with brilliant teamwork – like the Romans, or the Zulus. The success of these armies was largely down to the fact that they presented a united, and nearly impenetrable, shield wall to the enemy.

Used this way, a shield wasn't just a defensive weapon, but a battering ram that would smash the opposition into the ground. But it all depended on team work. An isolated Zulu warrior was as vulnerable as anyone else – it was when he locked shields with his brothers and charged forward with them that he became practically invincible.

In our battle against lust, the shield of faith is a key weapon in our armory. With it Paul says we "can extinguish all the flaming darts of the evil one."[105] Lust certainly comes at us like fiery arrows. So have your shield ready.

How can we swing the shield of faith into action then? It happens when your faith convinces you that what Jesus offers is more desirable than what the principalities and powers offer. There is an old Greek story about the Sirens – three seductive women who lured sailors to shipwreck on their island by their beautiful music. Only two heroes managed to resist the Sirens. One was Odysseus, who lashed himself to the mast of his boat so that he could hear the music, but wasn't able to respond to it and steer his ship onto the rocks. The second hero was Jason, who resisted the Sirens by preferring the music of Orpheus, who sang on his boat.

Jason's method of steering clear of trouble was much better than Odysseus'. Odysseus is like the guy who spends all his time wishing

---

[105] Ephesians 6:16

he could watch porno, but keeping himself from it simply by the strength of his will. Jason didn't even want the porno, because he had found something he liked more. This is how the shield of faith works.

Whenever we hear the siren voice of temptation and are drawn to it, but then turn our ears and hearts to the voice of Jesus and what he offers us, we are putting the shield in place. Every time we choose the way of righteousness rather than the way of sin because we have faith that righteousness is better the shield gets stronger. Faith is believing that what Jesus offers us is true, and is very, very good, even if we can't feel how it could be at the time.

But this isn't something we are meant to do on our own. The shield gets really strong only when it is locked in an impenetrable wall with the shields of our brothers and sisters in Christ. Christians are always meant to be part of a local church. You are meant to love your church. To be committed to it. To do the work in it you are meant to do. Each of us needs to be like one of those Roman or Zulu soldiers, determined to hold the line and play our part. Lone warriors tend to get hacked down, but even the guy who doesn't look that big or impressive can be part of a sin-smashing battering ram when he is locked into a shield wall.

None of us beats lust on our own. Those fiery darts can just come from too many directions at once. We need to be linked into an army that enables us to fight and win. You see, our own faith is strengthened and grows as we stand alongside other people of faith. So get your shield in place, and get into your place in the church.

The helmet of salvation

When you are getting plagued by lust it is easy to think that the most important part of your body is your gonads – but actually it is your brain. Think about it: If you didn't have a brain you wouldn't be able to think about your gonads! So you need to get your brain covered, and that's what a helmet is for.

Most of the time a helmet doesn't seem necessary. I used to do a lot of cycling and wearing a helmet felt a waste of time because it didn't do anything. All the other bits of kit I wore were useful every time I was on the bike – shoes, bike shorts, shirt – all were very necessary, but the helmet seemed a bit useless. When it was hot the helmet only made my head sweatier, but when it was cold the helmet didn't really offer any significant insulation. What was the point in wearing it? But one day I was in a race and had a bad crash. Going down a steep hill, too fast, in the rain, the bike went from underneath me and I ended up on my back in the road. I got some nasty scrapes and I also got a concussion. But that 'useless' helmet possibly saved my life.

A helmet usually doesn't seem necessary, but when you need it you really need it. And the only way to make sure you are wearing it when you need it is to wear it all the time.

Lust sometimes comes out of the blue. It can hit us out of nowhere and smack us down. It can be like getting whacked by a baseball bat. So you need a good helmet.

Paul says that the helmet we are to wear is "the helmet of salvation."[106] This is the best kind of helmet of all. It is going to protect your brain from the bumps of sin. Putting this bit of kit on happens when we understand who we really are in Christ. The world, the flesh and the devil will all tell you that you are just a mess of hormones, or just plumbing, or a piece of junk who might as well look at that porno or go and get laid. The helmet of salvation tells us who we *really* are – Sons of the King. And if we know who we are in Christ then we won't go looking for our identity in sex.

One way that an army in the heat of battle could tell who was on which side was by the helmets they were wearing. It is our headgear that gives us away. When I put on my bike helmet it says I am a cyclist. When a policeman puts on his cap it makes it clear who he is and the authority he bears. When you put on the helmet of salvation it makes it plain that you are in the Lord's army.

---

[106] Ephesians 6:17

Like his shield, a soldier's helmet wasn't purely defensive. If a fight is up close and personal you can use a helmet to smash another guy's face in. Head butt your enemy good and hard in the face and you're going to leave the impression of your helmet all over him. This is what we should do when lust comes calling. Keep that helmet of salvation on. Look at yourself in the mirror and remind yourself who you are – you are in Jesus' army and answerable to him. You are his son, a prince in his household, so you're not to go whoring after another master. The helmet of salvation is your sign of authority – that you are under the authority of Jesus, and that you carry authority as his representative on the earth. This means you have authority over the devil. As James puts it, "Submit yourselves to God. Resist the devil, and he will flee from you."[107] Wear a helmet, and go to war!

Some guys walk around like they are brain dead, with their heads uncovered and unprotected. When lust comes looking for them they fall at the first hit. Don't be this kind of idiot. Protect your brain. Keep your helmet on.

The sword of the Spirit

The last piece of kit in the armor of God is "the sword of the Spirit, which is the word of God."[108] This is a weapon with which you can fight!

What the Romans and Zulus both discovered was that a short sword (a short spear in the case of the Zulus) was more effective than a long one. The reason for this was that protected behind their shield wall, a short sword was much more maneuverable than a long one. It might *feel* safer to have a long sword and keep the enemy at a distance, but protected by a shield you don't want to fight this way – you want to get in close to the enemy and stuff him up the ribs with a short, sharp, and deadly sword thrust.

We should handle our Bibles the same way.

---

[107] James 4:7
[108] Ephesians 6:17

Your Bible shouldn't be something which you wave around ineffectually on the end of a long stick, hoping it will somehow strike its target. Instead it is something you need close at hand, and comfortable in your hand.

Paul tells his disciple Timothy that, "All Scripture is breathed out by God and profitable for teaching, for reproof, for correction, and for training in righteousness, that the man of God may be competent, equipped for every good work."[109] This is how the sword of the Spirit works – we learn how to use it in every situation so that we train ourselves in righteousness. As the Psalms tell us, it is by the word of God that we keep our way pure.[110]

This means we need to get to know our Bible, and this means reading it! It means that we know verses of scripture that can help us when we face temptation – the kind of verses I have quoted throughout this book, which warn us against temptation and promise us better things in Christ. For example, if you never read your Bible you will not know that it promises us that, "No temptation has overtaken you that is not common to man. God is faithful, and he will not let you be tempted beyond your ability, but with the temptation he will also provide the way of escape, that you may be able to endure it."[111] That is a good promise to know! It is a good one with which to stab the enemy when you are being tempted. It is the kind of promise that you can pray into aggressive action: "I know that I can beat this temptation, because God has promised a way out for me!"

But if we are going to wield this weapon effectively we need to be full of the Holy Spirit ourselves. Paul tells us to use the Sword of the Spirit while "praying at all times in the Spirit."[112] If the Spirit of God is not active in you, then the Bible is going to be a dead book to you – you might just as well try to fight off temptation with a copy of the Yellow Pages! So pray yourself full of the Spirit!

If you have never known what it is to be filled with the Spirit you need to have faith that it is God's desire for you that you do. How do

---

[109] 2 Timothy 3:16-17
[110] Psalm 119:9
[111] I Corinthians 10:13
[112] Ephesians 6:18

I know this? Because the Bible tells me so! Jesus told his disciples that the coming of the Spirit was "the promise of my Father"[113] and throughout the New Testament we see the impact of this promise. This wasn't just a promise for those first disciples but for all God's people for all of time, so get yourself filled!

The normal, Bible, way in which we receive the Spirit is when another Spirit-filled believer prays for us, and this is just one more reason why we need to get in rank in a good church. If you are to beat lust, then you need to be surrounded by other believers who can pray for you to know the empowering presence of the Spirit – and you should be praying for others in the same way.

Waging war in the full armor

Wearing all this kit takes some getting used to, and being in a fight is never easy. But if you start practicing putting the gear on, and taking a stand, you will get to the point where the principalities and powers no longer touch you. You will find freedom.

The fight against lust is a fight we should never fight alone. If you have a problem with lust you need to find some other soldiers to fight alongside, and a good leader to follow. In the Roman army soldiers would have fought shield to shield following the lead of their centurion. Find yourself a good centurion – a pastor or youth leader, someone you respect and can trust – and get stuck in behind them, watching how they fight the principalities and powers, and helping your fellow soldiers to do the same.

A posse of committed soldiers is not going to get distracted from their mission by anything. They are going to march straight on by every temptation. You need to learn to do the same – and you can. The fight against lust is a fight you can win.

---

[113] Luke 24:49

Printed in Great Britain
by Amazon.co.uk, Ltd.,
Marston Gate.